THE COMPLETE
ENCYCLOPEDIA OF
COCKTAILS

THE COMPLETE
ENCYCLOPEDIA OF
COCKTAILS

**Filled with traditional cocktails,
with and without alcohol**

SIMON POLINSKY

© 2002 Rebo International b.v.

This edition published 2002
by Hackberry Press
an imprint of Texas Bookman

Text: R&R, Australia
Production: R&R, Australia
Cover design: Minkowsky Graphics, Enkhuizen

ISBN 1-931040-13-3

Contents

1.	History of Spirit Distillation	6
2.	Distillation Process	10
3.	Types of Stills	11
4.	The Science of Cocktail Making	13
5.	The Base Spirits	16
	Whiskey	16
	Brandy	26
	Gin	29
	Tequila	32
	Rum	34
	Vodka	36
6.	Techniques	40
7.	A-Z of Cocktails	47
8.	Cocktail Index	318

1. History of Spirits and Distillation

In the middle ages spirit was known as "aqua vitae", a term which survives today in Swedish and Norwegian aquavit and Danish Akvavit. This was symptomatic, because the name means "water of life."

In ancient Greece, Aristotle wrote: "Sea water can be rendered potable by distillation. After it has been converted into humid vapours it returns to liquid." A Greek is said to have discovered this simply by noticing how steam condensed on the inner lid of a dish.

The principal remedies of the ancients were, as we know, wine and herbs. From the time of the Egyptians, great use was made of flowers, plants, and spices cooked, macerated or infused for pharmaceutical or culinary purposes. The healing perfumed liquid was preserved in airtight jars with wine or water. The science of distillation, if not continuously practised, crops up again and again in history. The distillates, as far as we know, were water and scents. The discovery of the distillation of alcohol was made by the Arabs in the early Middle Ages. In the tenth century, the philosopher Avicenna produced a complete description of the alembic, but did not mention alcohol - although it must have been discovered about that time. Like alchemy, the word "alcohol" derives from the Arabic.

A certain black powder was liquified, converted to vapour, allowed to solidify again, and then used as eye paint by the harem beauties. This was "kohl", which is in use throughout the Arab world today. And when the spirit of wine began to be distilled, the Arabic name for this distilled powder - "Al Koh'l" - was adopted, because of the similarity of the process.

In fact, we inherited the Arabian science of distillation by way of alchemy, which played a larger part in the medieval world. The earliest name of genuine importance in distillation is that of Arnau of Vilanove (d 1313), a Catalan professor at the University of Montpellier. He was probably the first to write about alcohol and his traits on wine and spirits was a handbook of the time. His pupil, Rainumdo Lulio (or Raymond Lull), was a philosopher and chemist who carried on with the experiments. "Eau-de-vie", Lulio wrote, is "an emanation of the divinity, an element newly revealed to men but hiden from antiquity, because the human race was then too young to need this beverage, destined to revive the energies of modern decrepitude." Arnau was more ecstatic. To him, the liquor was the long-sought panacea, the elixir of life itself, the dream of the alchemists. Although they never found what they were looking for - the secret of transmuting base metal into gold, or the elixir of everlasting life - the alchemists discovered a great many other things in the process. They developed the science of chemistry; and while they did not discover "aqua vitae", they used it extensively and bequeathed its uses to us.

To the general public, "aqua vitae" was a medicine and tasted like one. Another name for it was "aqua ardens" - firewater. The fruit and herbs with which the spirits were doctored helped to hide the taste as well as to heal the patients. When, later on, people began to think of brandies and liqueurs primarily as drinks, there was much experimenting with different plants to improve the flavor; and except in such favored regions as Cognac, Frenchmen were still tackling the same problem at the end of the eighteenth century. Then, in 1800, Adeem invented the process of rectification of rectifying - that is, a redistillation which removed the "mauvais gout." Unfortunately, it removed all taste, good as well as bad, and the French, who had been adding herbs and fruit concoctions to hide the nasty taste, had to restore them again to give flavor to the neutral spirit.

"Aqua vitae" was on sale in Italy in the Middle Ages. At about the same time, or a little earlier, it appeared in Ireland, gaelicized into "uisge beatha" and distilled from a barley beer. Variants of this name for the "water of life" persisted throughout the centuries, but in the end it was unquestionably whisky.

Scotch whisky originated in the Highlands. By the fifteenth century, it was a familiar drink there and was purely malt whisky. Gradually it seeped through to the Lowlands and the Scottish court.

The English at first preferred the fine French Cognac brandies miraculously distilled from the thin sharp wines of Charente. In early days, ships from the north used to put in at La Rochelle, principally to pick up salt. Then the inhabitants began to sell their wine as well; and afterward, to save space in the ships - and perhaps to avoid taxes - they began to boil down the wine, which travelled much better when it was thus metamorphosed. At first the idea was to restore the wine by adding water when it reached land again, but it was soon discovered to taste better as it was. A gentleman called Croix-Maron, who is supposed to have had a lot to do with the boiling down of the wine, is said to have remarked: "In cooking my wines, I have discovered their soul."

A report from 1688 says that very little wine of the Charente region could be sold abroad, both "when the white wines are converted to 'eau-de'vie', which is the customary thing, then the English and Danish fleets come to the ports of the Charente in search of it." So, by the date, the brandy of Cognac was established. The name "brandy" may well have come from the Germanic "Branntwein" - burnt wine. There are mentions of "brand wine" in English in 1622 and 1650.

It is interesting that much of the early distilling was done in the house, and the politest ladies were proficient in this domestic art, as common as cooking. Scotch whisky was at first almost entirely made at home: the best was for the Highland chiefs; the crofters mashed their surplus grain into whisky. When, in that mountainous and inaccessible country, the domestic stills were banned by the Hanoverian kings, and heavy taxes and duties began to be placed on the spirit, the distillers quite naturally took to the hills.

It is estimated that of the roughly half a million gallons of Scotch whisky being made annually in 1800, the amount made legally was approximately nil. Some 300,000 illegal gallons are said to have eluded the excise men and flowed down over the border into England year after year. At one time there were two hundred illicit stills in the famous glen of Glenlivet, where perhaps the finest unblended whisky in the world is made today.

The Scottish distillers were defiant men who brewed their illegal potions quite openly. All that was necessary was to choose a defendable glen, and then go about armed to the teeth. In 1823, the English government lowered the duty on whisky in order to encourage the open and legal distillation of good spirit. Yet the illicit stills were so well established that when a daredevil named George Smith came to Glenlivet itself and set up a legal distillery, he was considered to have shown great effrontery. His memoirs tell nothing of how he made his whisky, but they do tell the secret of his success. He hired the toughest men he could find, and by standing watch in turn with them around the clock he saved his still from being burned out, the fate that befell the few others as bold as himself. Smith's foothold in Glenlivet was the beginning of the end. The sad decline in illegal distilling can be read in the statistics of illicit stills detected in Scotland; in 1834, 177; in 1854, 73; in 1864, 19; in 1874, 6. Whisky-runners were a dying race, like the romantic highwaymen of the previous century.

American whiskey (the word is spelled whisky in Canada, England and Scotland, whiskey in the United States and Ireland) began to be made in the eighteenth century. Distilling of rye and barley grains had become so strong a habit by the year 1794 that such interferences as taxation and control were resented to the point of armed revolt - this was the year of the Whiskey Rebellion in Pennsylvania. The distillers, losing the fight, moved west in large numbers, preferring the Indians to revenue men. A few years before, in Bourbon County, Kentucky, they had started making corn whiskey; with the arrival of the refugees from the east, the trade prospered. At first corn whiskey was made to reduce the carrier's load; the pack-horses winding down the narrow mountain trails of Kentucky could carry only 4 bushels of corn each; when the corn was distilled to whiskey, they could carry the equivalent of 24 bushels. This corn whiskey took the name "Bourbon" from Bourbon County.

There was another incentive for home distilling, and that was the whisky price in Kentucky. In 1782, about the time when the first Bourbon stills were set up, the price fixed by the court in Jefferson County, Kentucky, was 15 dollars a half-pint and 240 dollars a gallon. The Indians had already set the example, making a corn spirit they called Nohelick (the Apaches, further west in undiscovered territory, were brewing their Teeswin from boiled corn), and the settlers pitched in. The first may have been Elijah Craig. At any rate, that intrepid Baptist preacher "considered it as honourable a business as any. Even preachers did not deem it derogatory to their high calling to lend their countenance to its manufacture and engage in it themselves, or drink a little for the stomach's sake."

Adam's process of rectification eventually set off a complete revolution in the manufacture of spirits. Cognac (which even now is never rectified, but is pot-distilled by the ancient method derived from the alembic) changed its manner of exportation some three-quarters of a century ago as a consequence of the growing competition from rectified spirits. Traditionally shipped in barrels, it began to be exported in bottles, so that the distillers and shippers could be sure of having full control over the liquid they were selling - sent abroad in casks, it was increasingly likely that it would be stretched and adulterated at the end of its journey. One important consequence was that the brandy began to be called after the little rivertown from which it was shipped, and for the first time it was known as Cognac.

Rum - the sugar-cane spirit of the West Indies - had a riotous history in those islands. It was the traditional drink of the fighting men along the sea lanes of the empire-builders - and if the sailors did not get their issue of rum, there was danger of mutiny. The blaxing cane-juice brew was also the drink of the western American Colonies and, in one sense, fired them to revolt and form an independent United States - for England's taxing of rum was resented at least as bitterly as her taxing of tea. Even more romantic was the connection of rum with the pirates of the Spanish Main. In the coves of Barbados, Jamaica, and the other islands, the privateers hove to for concealment - and a fresh load of rum.

We drink - by and large - rather tamed rum today. Once again it is rectification that has brought about the revolution. By repeated redistilling, all by-products can be eliminated from any base liquid - in many a light modern rectified rum little of the lustiness of the pungent cane is left. These light rums are the Puerto Rican and Cuban - different from the heavier, pungent, sweeter liquors of Demerara and Jamaica, and more to the modern taste.

It is in the vast popularity of gin and vodka that the true effects of rectification appear. Both are, fundamentally, spirits made neutral by rectification, then - in the case of gin - reflavored. The persisting predilection for gin may be called "the vogue of the Martini." During Prohibition, complex mixtures of alcohol appear all over North America and spread their influence over the world. These mixtures were known as cocktails. Evolving perhaps from cold punches or mint juleps, they certainly developed and multiplied as they did because illicit synthetic "bath tub" gins needed to be well-disguised by other, less disgusting flavors. Nowadays the cocktail - once so complex - grows simpler and simpler.

The overwhelming preference is for the Martini - simply gin with a touch of vermouth, a concoction which is only possible when the basic ingredients are good.

Vodka is the latest craze. Originally a Russian, Polish, Balkan, Lithuanian and Estonian spirit, it is now made from grain in the United States and in England, France and elsewhere in Europe. The Smirnoff vodka formula bought by an American firm in 1939 from a White Russian refugee started this post-war fashion.

2. Distillation Process

Spirits are made in specially designed machines called stills. As the base liquid in the still warms up, the first vapor that forms is methyl alcohol. Because alcohol boils at a lower temperature than water, it is possible to vaporize nearly all the alcohol in the base liquid leaving mostly water behind. This is the type of alcohol used in substances such as fuel anti-freeze. It's lethal stuff and modern distillation methods first remove all the methyl alcohol.

After all the vaporized methyl alcohol is removed, ethyl alcohol - the alcohol in the spirits you drink - begins vaporizing along with some water. The vaporized mixture is carefully collected by rapid condensation until the later stages of distillation, when it becomes more water than alcohol.

Typically, distillers must re-distill the base liquid at least once and sometimes 3 or 4 times.

Besides alcohol and water, base liquor contains many other aromatic and flavorful elements called 'congeners'. These add richness and complexity to a finished spirit. It's the distiller's challenge to capture them without including any undesirable impurities.

If the spirit is to have a neutral taste, as in Vodka and Gin, the condensed vapor - called the distillate - must be re-distilled or rectified after collection. Rectification is simply a technical term for repeated distillation that removes all traces of flavor from the pure spirit.

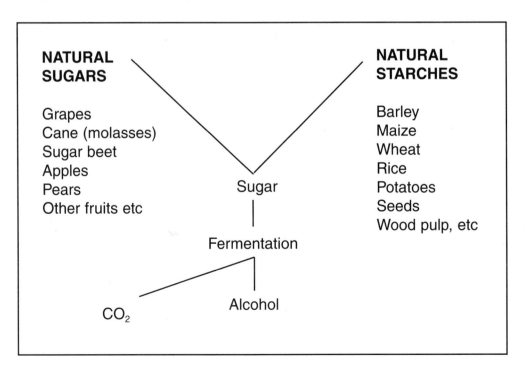

NATURAL SUGARS

Grapes
Cane (molasses)
Sugar beet
Apples
Pears
Other fruits etc

NATURAL STARCHES

Barley
Maize
Wheat
Rice
Potatoes
Seeds
Wood pulp, etc

Sugar

Fermentation

CO_2

Alcohol

3. Types of stills

THE POT STILL

The POT STILL is the traditional tool of the distiller. Its basic design has changed little since the days when medieval monks distilled spirits for medicinal purposes. It's usually made of copper in the shape of an onion.

Even today, the pot may be heated by a fire burning below it. More often, however, it is encircled by gas operated warming coils. The heated liquid inside the still vaporizes and passes through a spout to a condenser, where the spirit is liquefied and collected. The process is slow because only small quantities are made at one time in each pot still. Today, pot stills are used for higher priced spirits known for their special rich flavors. These include Malt Scotches from Scotland, Cognac Brandy from France, Irish Whiskies and most dark rums. They may also be used for rectification in making Gin or other 'white' spirits.

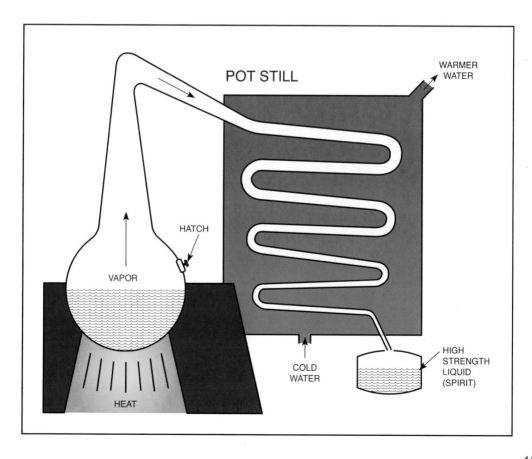

POT STILL

WARMER WATER

HATCH

VAPOR

HEAT

COLD WATER

HIGH STRENGTH LIQUID (SPIRIT)

THE PATENT STILL

The PATENT STILL is also called the 'Continuous' or 'Coffey' still. It was invented in 1831 by A. Coffey, an Irishman.

It can be used almost continuously day and night, without the constant attention required by a pot still. A steady stream of liquid enters the still at the top of a copper column where it is heated to steam and vaporized. The distillate then passes through condensing coils into another column where it is vaporized by steam and rectified. Specially designed plates inside the still ensure that the correct proportions of drinkable elements are collected.

The advantages of this system are many. Large quantities of spirits are produced at relatively low cost. In addition, the patent still is more successful at purifying alcohol than the pot still.

Depending on how often the spirit is passed through the still, the end product may taste neutral like Vodka, or have much flavor, like grain whiskies.

With the patent still, a famous brand of spirit may be made anywhere in the world. The product of the pot still depends on the local water and often specific operating conditions for its unique flavor.

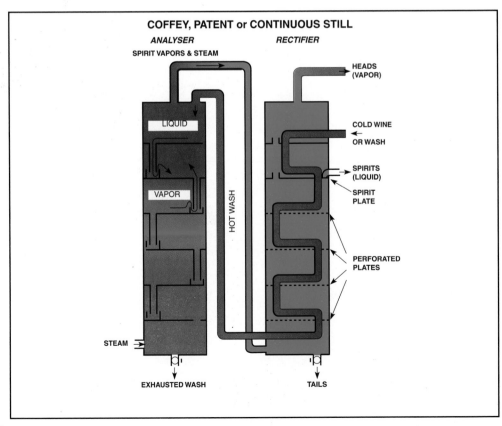

COFFEY, PATENT or CONTINUOUS STILL

ANALYSER
SPIRIT VAPORS & STEAM

RECTIFIER

HEADS (VAPOR)

LIQUID

COLD WINE OR WASH

SPIRITS (LIQUID)

SPIRIT PLATE

VAPOR

HOT WASH

PERFORATED PLATES

STEAM

EXHAUSTED WASH

TAILS

4. The Science of Cocktail Making

THE BASE

This is the fundamental and distinguishing ingredient of the cocktail and must always comprise more than 50% of the entire volume. Indeed, with a few rare exceptions, it should constitute 75% of total volume upwards. Strictly speaking, the base must always consist of a single spiritous liquor and this one liquor, being the predominant ingredient, determines the type of cocktail: Gin for Martinis, Whisky for Manhattans, Rum for Daiquiris. Within certain limits, however, it is possible to combine two (perhaps even more, but this is dangerous) liquors as a base. For example, Rye and Bourbon Whiskies, while differing decidedly in flavor, have the same essential characteristics and may be used pretty much either interchangeably or in combination as a base. Gin and White Cuban also blend very satisfactorily and may be used in combination. On the other hand, the indiscriminate mixture of three or five different liquors is practically certain to destroy the distinguishing flavor and aroma of all produce, a result about as palatable as a blend of castor oil and gasoline.

THE MODIFYING AGENT

It is this ingredient, in combination with the base of spiritous liquor, which characterises the cocktail. The flavor of the modifier itself should never predominate but should always remain submerged. The Gin Cocktail should still remain definitely and recognisably a Gin Cocktail. The Whisky Cocktail a Whisky Cocktail, but the modifier should add that elusive "je ne sais quoi" which makes the cocktail a smooth, fragrant, inspirational delight and not a mere drink of Gin or Whisky.

In general, modifying agents may be divided into three classes:

AROMATIC - including the aromatic wines, such as French and Italian Vermouth, Dubonnet, Byrrh, etc. and bitters of various types.

Fruit Juices - orange, lemon, lime, etc, with or without sugar.

Miscellaneous - "smoothing" agents - sugar, cream, eggs, etc.

All of these modifiers, particularly the aromatics and, above all, the bitters must be used with discretion. Just how far you should go with each agent you will learn by experience, relying both on your palate and on the comments of the customer. With a bitters, a safe rule, particularly if bitters are used in conjunction with an aromatic wine, is no more than 2 or 3 dashes per drink. In using cream or eggs, remember that you are preparing a drink and not a meal.

A safe rule for these miscellaneous smoothing agents is an absolute maximum of half a whole egg. 1 tablespoon heavy cream or 1 teaspoon of sugar to each drink.

Cocktail Ingredients

Base	Brandy, Gin, Rum, Whiskey, Tequila, Vodka		
Modifying	**Aromatics**	**Wines**	Dry Vermouth Sweet Vermouth Dubonnet Sherry
		Bitters	Angostura Abbot's Aged Bronekamp Peychaud
		Citric Bitters	Orange Lime
		Miscellaneous	Amer Picon Campari Fernert Branca
	Fruit Juices		Apple Apricot Grapefruit Lemon Lime Orange Passion Fruit Pear Peach Pineapple Plum Raspberry Tomato

SPECIAL COLORING AND FLAVORING AGENTS

These include all the various cordials or liqueurs, as well as non-alcoholic fruit syrups. They should never dominate and overpower the flavor of the base. These special flavoring agents are to be measured by drops or dashes.

Modifying	Miscellaneous	Cream Egg Milk Milk (coconut) Milk (soya) Sugar
Color Flavoring	Syrups, Cordials	Grenadine Orgeat Mint Raspberry
	Liqueurs	Advocaat Anisette Amaretto Apricot Brandy Baileys Benedictine Chartreuse Cointreau Creme de Drambule Galliano

5. The Base Spirits

1. WHISKEYS

Scotch Whisky

The term scotch means that the whisky was distilled and matured in the country whose name it bears. Scotch is the most complex of whiskeys, with unusual combinations of sweetness and dryness. The sweetness coming from the primary grain, malted barley, which is the singular ingredient that is mostly associated with scotch. The dryness comes from the smoky qualities that are derived by drying the malted barley in kilns fired with peat from local bogs and the water which runs through the heather and peat moors.

Scotch is aged in a variety of barrels: used port, sherry, bourbon, etc. which add to the complexity and variety of scotches.

All of the largest selling scotches are blended, not only from malts but also from the lighter and more neutral tasting grain whiskeys made from unmalted barley or, more often, corn. The object of blending is to iron out the rough edges of individual whiskies and produce something that will appeal to (or be acceptable to) a broader taste. The blender usually has a wide variety of malts available from all four regions of scotch malts.

Like wines - and many other drinks - the single malts of Scotland are grouped by region. As with wines, these regions offer a guideline rather than a rule. Within Bordeaux, a particular Pomerol, for example, might have a richness more reminiscent of Burgundy; similar comparisons can be made in Scotland. The regions in Scotland have their origins in the regulation of licenses and duties, but they do also embrace certain characteristics.

The Lowlands

The Lowlands tend to produce whiskeys in which the softness of the malt itself is more evident, untempered by Highland peatiness or coastal brine and seaweed. The Lowlands is defined by a line following old country boundaries and running from the Clyde estuary to the river Tay. The line swings north of Glasgow and Dumbarton and runs to Dundee and Perth.

The Highlands

The Highlands is by far the bigger region, and inevitably embraces wide variations. The western part of the Highlands, at least on the mainland, has only a few, scattered distilleries, and it is difficult to generalize about their character. If they have anything in common, it is a rounded, firm, dry character, with some peatiness. The far north of the Highlands has several whiskies with a notably heathery, spicy character, probably deriving both from the soil and the coastal location of all distilleries. The more sheltered East Highlands and the Midlands of Scotland (sometimes described as the South Highlands) have a number of notably fruity whiskies.

None of these Highland areas are officially regarded as regions, but the area

between them is known as Speyside, universally acknowledged as a heartland of malt distillation. This area, between the cities of Inverness and Aberdeen, sweeps from granite mountains down to fertile countryside, where barley is among the crops. It is the watershed of a system of rivers, the principal among which is the Spey. Although it is not precisely defined, Speyside is commonly agreed to extend at least from the river Findhorn to the Deveron.

The Speyside single malts are noted in general for their elegance and complexity, and often a refined smokiness. Beyond that, they have two extremes: the big, sherryish type and the lighter, more subtle style.

Within Speyside, the river Livet is so famous that its name is borrowed by some whiskies from far beyond its glen. Only one may call itself The Glenlivet; only two more are produced in the valley, and a further one in the parish. These are all delicate malts, and it could be more tentatively argued that other valleys have malts that share certain characteristics.

The Highland region includes a few good coastal and island malts, but one peninsula and just one island have been of such historical importance in the industry that they are each regarded as being regions in their own right.

Campbelltown

On the peninsula called the Mull of Kintyre, Campbeltown once had about 30 distilleries. Today, it has only three. One of these, Springbank, produces two different single malts. This apparent contradiction is achieved by the use of a lightly peated malt in one and a smokier kilning in the other. The Campbeltown single malts are very distinctive, with a briny character. Although there are only three of them, they are still considered to represent a region in their own right.

Islay

Pronounced "eye-luh", this is the greatest of whisky islands; much of it deep with peat, lashed by the wind, rain and sea in the inner Hebrides. It is only 25 miles long, but has no fewer than eight distilleries, although not all are working. Its single malts are noted for their seaweedy, iodine-like, phenolic character. A dash of Islay malt gives the unmistakable tang of Scotland to many blended whiskies.

Single Malts are the most natural of spirits formed, more than any other, by their environment. For that same reason, they are the most individualistic. No other Spirit offers such diversity of character nor epitomizes the distiller's art, more than Single Malts.

The term SINGLE has a very clear and precise meaning. It indicates that the whisky was made in only one distillery, and has not been blended with any from elsewhere.

The term MALT indicates the raw material: barley malt, and no other grain or fermentable material; infused with water, fermented with yeast and distilled in a pot.

The term SCOTCH means that the whisky was distilled and matured in the country whose name it bears. Outside Britain, there are two single malts (but no Scotch) made in Ireland. There are also three or four single malts (but no Scotch) made in Japan.

A SINGLE MALT SCOTCH must fulfill all three requirements. It must be the product of only one distillery; it must be made exclusively from barley malt; and it must be made in Scotland.

There has been the odd occasion when the product of one run of the still has been aged in identical casks, then bottled. This has been described as a "Single/Single". That is not the normal procedure. Although a single malt always comes from one distillery, whisky from half-a-dozen production batches over a two-year period, aged in different casks, might be married in wood for several weeks and then fed into one bottling run. The age on the bottle will represent the youngest whisky inside.

Some single malts are labeled as "Pure Malt." However, this term is also often used to indicate a vatting together of malt whiskies made in several distilleries. This type of whisky is technically known as vatted malt. It may also be labeled simply as a "Malt Whisky" or "Scotch Malt Whisky." Although such bottlings are perfectly legitimate and often excellent products, their labels usually identify only the brand-owner or blender, and not the distilleries.

A blended Scotch commonly contains about 40 percent malt; the odd one contains more than 60 percent.

The cheaper blends contain much less. The deluxe blends are likely to contain a good proportion of well-matured malt, which is why some carry an age statement. Once again the age statement reflects the age of the youngest whisky. All single malts are individuals, in some cases as distinct from each other as they are from the blends they inhabit. But before looking at the variables that conspire to produce such a diverse family, a brief reminder of the processes used in the creation of all malts might be helpful.

MALTING: Barley has to be partially germinated before it can release its fermentable sugars. It is soaked in water until it begins to sprout, then this is arrested by drying the grains over heat. This steeping and drying process is called malting. Traditionally, the Scots dried their malt over a peat fire, which gives Scotch its characteristic smokiness. A proportion of peat is still burned during malting.

MASHING: To complete the conversion of starch into fermentable sugars, the malt (which has been milled after malting) is mixed with warm water in a vessel called a mashtum. The liquid drained off, is known as wort.

FERMENTATION: The sugars in the wort are now turned into alcohol during fermentation, which takes place with the addition of yeast, in a fermentation vessel.

DISTILLATON: This is the boiling of the fermented wort, in a pot-still. Because alcohol boils more rapidly than water, the spirit is separated as a vapor and collected as it condenses back to alcohol.

MATURATION: All malts are matured in oak barrels, for a legal minimum of three years, though usually much longer.

A single malt is distilled in traditional vessels that resemble a copper kettle or pot. These are known as pot-stills. Most other types of whisky are made predominantly from other grains, in a more modern system: a continuous still, shaped like a column.

Much of the flavor of the malt is retained in pot distillation because this Old Fashioned system is inherently inefficient. A column system can distill more thoroughly, but makes for a less flavorful spirit. Blended Scotch whiskeys contain a proportion of pot-still malt, leavened with continuous-still whisky made from cheaper, unmalted grains.

The pot-still is a vessel shaped by a coppersmith, and in no two distilleries is it identical. Some Scottish malt distilleries trace their history from the late 1700s, and many from the early and mid 1800s. Over the years, each distillery has been reluctant to change the shape of its stills. As they wear out, they are replaced by new ones of the same design. If the last still was dented, the distillery may get the same depression hammered into the new still.

The reason for this is that every variation in the shape of the still affects the character of the product. A small, squat still produces a heavy, oily, creamy spirit. In a large still, some of the vapors condense before they have left the vessel, fall back and are redistilled. This means that tall stills produce lighter, cleaner spirits.

Irish Whiskey

In the 6th Century AD, Irish monks journeyed to the Middle East and it is thought that it was there they observed how the alembic was used to distil perfume. On returning to Ireland they invented their own version - the 'Pot Still'. This they used to create a new spirit known as 'Uisce Beatha' - 'The Water of Life'

BARLEY - MALTED AND UNMALTED: Irish Whiskey is made either from malted barley or from a mixture of malted and unmalted barley and other cereals. In Ireland the malt is dried in closed Kilns unlike in Scotland, where malt is dried over open peat fires. This, the malting process used for Irish Whiskey, not only avoids a smoky taste but also ensures a smooth and natural flavor.

MILLING: Precise amounts of barley and other cereals are ground and then mixed with pure water in a large vessel called a 'mash run'.

PUREST WATER: From the underground springs, in bubbling streams and fast-flowing rivers Ireland is blessed with an abundance of clear, pure water.

FERMENTATION: The starches in the mash are converted into a sugary liquid 'wort'. This is separated from the residual grains and pumped into the 'wash backs' where yeast converts the sugars in the wort to low strength alcohol or 'wash'.

THREE SEQUENTIAL DISTILLATIONS: The art of distillation enables the creation of new whiskey for 'wash'. This is the heart of the process with the wash being heated in large copper pot stills of traditional design. In Ireland whiskey is obtained only after three separate distillations, each sequence resulting in a further process of purification.

At the first stage a distillate named 'low wines' is obtained. This full flavored product called 'feints' requires one further distillation which is carried out in a spirit still. Thus, through a repeated sequence of distillations, a final spirit of light and delicate character is obtained. It is this new whiskey which, after maturation, will become Irish Whiskey.

MATURING IN OAK CASKS: The maturing whiskey is stored for years in vast, dark, aromatic warehouses. Here it rests in fine oak casks, some of which have been used previously for sherry. While the whiskey matures, there is a complex interaction between the whiskey, natural wood extracts, and the air which 'breathes' through the wood of the cask, giving a superb, mellow bouquet to the whiskey.

American Whiskey

Blended American Whiskey is a broad category of spirits that is produced by the distillate of a fermented grain mash which is aged and then blended. There are whiskeys made in Pennsylvania, Tennessee, Virginia, Kentucky, etc., all in different manners and/or processes. The most famous American Whiskey, of course, are bourbon whiskies.

Bourbon is America's native spirit, with a history and tradition steeped in the cultures of the earliest settlers. This unique American product has continually evolved and been refined over the past 200 plus years.

Among the first settlers who brought their whiskey making traditions to this country were the Scotch-Irish of Western Pennsylvania. Although whiskey was produced throughout the colonies (George Washington was among the noted whiskey producers of the time), these settlers of Pennsylvania are where bourbon's roots began.

To help finance the revolution, the Continental Congress put a tax on whiskey production. So incensed were the settlers of Western Pennsylvania that they refused to pay. To restore order to the ensuing "Whiskey Rebellion" of 1791 to 1794, Washington was forced to send the Continental Army to quell the uprising. This turned out not to be as easy as Washington thought it might be. To save the government from a potentially embarrassing political situation and to avoid further troubles with the very tough and stubborn Scotch-Irish settlers, Washington made a settlement with them, giving incentives for those who would move to Kentucky (at that time part of Virginia). The significance of this is that the early whiskey was made primarily from rye, this was about to change with their move and "Bourbon" would be born.

The Governor of Virginia, Thomas Jefferson, offered pioneers sixty acres of land in Kentucky if they would build a permanent structure and raise "native corn." No family could eat sixty acres worth of corn a year and it was too perishable and bulky to transport for sale; if it were turned into whiskey, both problems evaporated.

This corn based whiskey, which was a clear distillate, would become "bourbon" only after two coincidentally related events happened. The French, having at that time their own territories in North America, assisted in the War of Independence against the British. In acknowledgment of this, French names were subsequently used for new settlements or counties.

In the Western part of Virginia, the then county of Kentucky, was subdivided in 1780 and again in 1786. One of these subdivisions was named Bourbon County, after the French Royal House. Kentucky became a state in 1792 and Bourbon one of its counties.

Being on the Ohio River, the town of Marysville became a primary shipping port. Bourbon County thus became associated with the shipping of Whiskey.

The name of the spirit became synonymous because of this and one other event.

Although Evan Williams, in 1783, might have been the first commercial distiller in Louisville, Bourbon is sometimes considered to have begun with the Reverend Elijah Craig from Bourbon County. The legend goes that he was a might thrifty and used old barrels to transport his whiskey to market in New Orleans. He

charred the barrels before filling them, thus after his whiskey made the long trip to market, it had "mellowed" and taken on a light caramel color from the oak. Being from Bourbon County he started calling the whiskey "Bourbon". Interestingly today, there is no whiskey produced in Bourbon County.

In 1964, a congressional resolution protected the term "Bourbon" and only since then has the product been defined. The basic elements of Bourbon are that it must be a minimum of two years old, at least 80° (proof) and be made from a mash of at least 51% corn. It must be aged in charred new oak barrels. 99% of Bourbon Whiskey comes from Kentucky, but it doesn't have to, the "law" does not stipulate origin. Most consider the unique limestone spring water found in Kentucky the only water with that "just right" combination of minerals suitable enough for the finest Bourbons.

The next stage for the Bourbon producers is how the elements of production, storage, aging and bottling are handled.

Bourbons vary in style, philosophy and approach to production. If the mix of small grains in the mash changes, or the yeast strain used is different, so is the product. Many distill and age their whiskey at a different proof. Some crack the corn, some roll it. There are those that pay detailed attention to every detail from the growing and preparation of the grain to the proper rack house barrel rotation. In all bourbons you can find a unique point of difference and it is these subtle differences in the end product that beg study and comparison.

It is also this great variety of possibilities that make Bourbon whiskey one of the most interesting classifications of distilled spirits to explore.

Canadian Whisky

Canadian whisky is often offered to the drinker who has ordered "a rye." Some Canadian whiskies are even designated as rye on the label. This is an accurate, but confusing description. Whatever their labels say, all Canadian whiskies are of the same style. The classic method of production is to blend rye and perhaps other whiskies, with relatively neutral spirit. These are, indeed rye whiskies - but as blends. They are quite different from the traditional straight rye of the United States. That is the original "rye."

The best Canadian whiskies have at least some of the spicy, bitter-sweet character of rye, lightened with the blending spirit. In some instances, this too is distilled from rye but the raw material hardly matters, since it is rectified close to neutrality. More often, the blending spirit is made from corn.

A further component of the palate is a dash of the vanilla sweetness to be found in Bourbon. This may result from a proportion of Bourbon-type whisky having been used in the blend, or it may derive from the wood used in aging. Such is the pungency of straight rye and Bourbon that their characteristics are powerfully evident in the palate of a good Canadian whisky, despite its being a very dilute blend.

There is as little as three percent of straight whisky in some Canadians, more often four or five, but not as much as ten. This dash of flavor is counterpointed with the lightness of body provided by the far greater proportion of the neutral spirit.

One characteristic of many Canadian whiskies is their use of rye that has been malted. This provides a characteristic smoothness and fullness of flavor. Unmalted ryes are also used. Most blends include more than one rye whisky, and for this purpose a single distillery may produce several. The character and weight of these will vary according to the mash bill and distillation methods.

The mash bill for a rye whisky being produced for blending may also include more than one rye whisky, and for this purpose a single distillery may produce several. The character and weight of these will vary according to the mash bill and distillation methods.

The mash bill for a rye whisky being produced for blending may also include a small portion of barley malt, or perhaps some corn. The proportion of these ingredients can be varied to produce ryes of differing characters.

Canadian distilleries also produce their own Bourbon-type whiskies for blending purposes. They also make corn whiskies, and even distill unmalted barley, again to produce components for their blends.

The biggest producers, Seagram's, have half a dozen distilleries in Canada, using several different yeasts, and making more than 50 different straight whiskies for blending.

A large number of these will go into some of the more complex blends, and general Canadian practice is to use perhaps 20 different whiskies. Even the least complex blend will probably contain 15 whiskies, built around six or seven basic types.

The changes are also rung in the extent to which the various whiskies for blending are aged. In the case of rye, aging tends not only to smoothen the whisky but also to make it heavier. This effect is more evident if the rye is aged as a straight - and that raises another variable.

The extent to which whisky is aged before or after blending is a matter on which there are different and passionate schools of thought in Canada.

2. BRANDY

Some historians credit the Chinese with discovering the art of turning fruit wine or grain-based mash into a higher alcohol, purer beverage. Others claim the Egyptians were the creators of distillation. It's possible that both cultures were experimenting with distillation in roughly the same period.

Whatever the case, we know for certain that the Moors first established distillation in Europe during their occupation of southern Spain from the 8th century to the late 15th century. The Spaniards of the period were skilled winemakers and started using the pot stills that were left behind by the Moors.

Within a century, brandies made from fermented grapes and other fruits spread across continental Europe.

"Brandy" is derived from brandywijn, a word of Dutch origin for "burnt". Created in a still to leave the water and remove the alcoholic vapor which then turns back into liquid form as it cools. In other languages too, it is the burning that is the essential feature.

In theory distillation is the simplest of physical processes. It is based on the fact that alcohol and water boil at different temperatures, water at 100°C, alcohol at 78.3°C. If a fermented liquid is heated, the vapor containing the alcoholic constituents is released first. It can then be trapped and cooled, then condensed to an alcoholic liquid.

The process was probably first observed by the Arabs, who carried the torch of science during the Dark Ages. We still use their words "al-ambiq" (alembic) for the still, "al-kuhl" (alcohol) for the distillate. Originally, the object was to produce medicinal properties, but it was soon discovered that the use of an appropriate raw material produced a drinkable liquid, a "water of life", aqua vitae. But the raw materials were generally so impure that the alcohol could only be consumed with safety if it had been repeatedly redistilled, which removed most of the essential characteristics of the original raw material as well.

The biggest breakthrough came in the 16th and early 17th centuries. It was found that distilling the sharp white wines that were produced on the slopes overlooking the little town of Cognac in western France, resulted in spirits that after as few as two passes through the stills, produced an eminently drinkable brandy, especially if aged for a few years in oak casks. It has proved to be an unbeatable formula.

The next essential in making fine brandy is the speed of distillation: the slower, the gentler, the more effectively the aromatic elements in the raw material are detached with the alcohol, the better. It is rather like stewing fruit: the lower the flame on the stove, the more intense the aromas released and the more thoroughly is the residue drained of them. Indeed, the Cognacais like to describe their method of distillation as (speeded-up) evaporation.

They are right: the vapors should contain as high a proportion as possible of the congeners, the hundreds of organic chemical compounds which are extracted with the alcohol. Some of these are undesirable, bringing with them rank and unpleasant aromas and have to be removed. This entails a close control over distillation process to remove the "heads", the first vapors emerging from the still, which contain the bulk of these undesirable elements, and then the "tails" which will simply be too feeble, without the requisite alcoholic concentration.

At the other extreme are the continuous stills, invented early in the 19th century by, and named after, an Irishman, Coffey. This still can concentrate wine 10 or more times up to the normal industrial maximum of 96.6%.

This fast, continuous process saves heat (pot-stills have to be reheated between each batch), is highly productive - and can be highly destructive of all the elements which make brandy interesting.

Newly distilled brandy tastes raw, oily and unappetizing. The key to its final quality is a more or less lengthy sojourn in oak casks. The choice of wood was originally accidental: oak happened to be the most easily available for making the casks required by the pioneering distillers. They were, of course, accustomed to using wood to mature and market their wines.

Because brandy, like wine, is a product of the grape, oak has proved suitable for maturing it. But there are many varieties of oak and as with so many aspects of brandy making, local practices differ so widely that only a few generalizations can be offered as applying to the whole range of brandies.

Most of the qualities which make oak so suitable are physical. For whatever the chemical qualities of the wood and the reactions they induce when in prolonged contact with the spirit, it is the porosity of the cask which allows the brandy to have steady, limited access to the air. The brandy gradually absorbs the oxygen required to oxidize and thus soften the raw spirit.

3. GIN

When we think of gin we think of England and her former colonies. The actual origins of gin can be traced to 17th century Holland. Dr. Franciscus de La Boie invented gin in 1650. He was a medical professor at the University of Leyden and was more widely known as Dr. Sylvius. As was with many other spirits, gin was originally intended to be used as a medicine. Dr. Sylvius was seeking an inexpensive, but effective diuretic to use in the treatment of kidney disorders. He mixed oil of juniper berries with grain alcohol, both of which have diuretic properties. He called his new medical concoction "genever", from the French word for juniper.

What made the recipe so revolutionary, was not the use of juniper, it had been used before in dozens of liqueur formulas, but the choice of grain alcohol. Until Dr. Sylvius, most beverage alcohol had been made from grapes or other fruit. In other words, brandies. While the Scotch and Irish were making whiskies from grain, they tempered them with years of aging in wooded casks. Unaged grain spirits, at least those produced with 17th century technology, were considered too harsh for human consumption. But genever tasted good and it was relatively inexpensive to produce.

At the same time, English soldiers, who were fighting on the continent, were introduced to what they termed "Dutch Courage." They returned to England with a preference for this new drink, and the population at large soon grew fond of this palatable yet inexpensive spirit, so much so that it eventually became identified as the national drink of England. It was the English, of course, that shortened the name to "Gin."

Gin was also quite popular with the English foreign service in the "colonies." It mixed naturally with quinine (tonic water) which was used as a profilacsis to nullify the effects of malaria. Even today it's easy to conjure up an image of the British colonial officers sitting on a wide veranda sipping a gin and tonic while surveying his vast dominion.

London Dry and other styles

The dry gin that London distillers eventually developed is very different from the Holland or geneva gin still made by the Dutch, which is heavy-bodied and strongly flavored with a pronounced malty taste and aroma.

London dry gin appeared soon after the continuous still was invented in 1831.

This new still made a purer spirit possible, encouraging English distillers to try an unsweetened or dry style. Sugars had been used to mask the rough and unpleasant flavors that could show up in older pot still production.

Originally, the phrase "London dry gin" specified a geographic location; that the gin was made in or near London. Now, the term is considered to be generic and is used to describe a style of gin, (in fact, Beefeater is now the only gin distilled in London) and virtually every gin on the market uses the term "dry".

Gin is the distillate of a grain mash with various flavoring agents. It gets its primary flavor from juniper berries, but many other herbs and spices go into the make-up. The botanicals come from all over the world: cardamom from Sri Lanka, cassia bark from Vietnam, orange peel from Spain, coriander seed from the Czech Republic, angelica root from Germany. Most of the juniper berries themselves are imported from Italy. There are also dozens of other possible ingredients. Each distiller has his own secret formula and no two gin brands are exactly alike.

Production

The vast majority of this unaged spirit (federal regulations do not permit any age claims for gin, vodka and other neutral spirits) is either English dry gin or American dry gin. The English version uses 75% corn, 15% barley and 10% other grains for the mash. The fermentation process is similar to that of whiskey.

Following fermentation the resulting liquid is distilled and rectified through a column still, producing a pure spirit of at least 90°. The liquid is then redistilled with the many flavoring agents. Methods vary from producer to producer.

Some combine the botanicals with the spirit and distil the mixture, while others suspend the botanicals above the spirit in the still and let the vapors pass through the many flavoring agents. The spirit that comes off is reduced to bottling strength, anywhere from 80° to 97°.

American gin is produced using one of two standard methods: distilling and compounding. Distilled gin is primarily made by adding the flavoring agents during a continuous process. There are two fairly similar methods of achieving this - direct distillation or redistillation.

In direct distillation the fermented grain mash is pumped into the still. Then it is heated and the spirit vapors pass through a "gin head", a sort of percolator basket filled with juniper, herbs and other natural ingredients. It picks up the delicate flavoring agents as it passes through and then condenses into a high proof gin. Water is added to bring the product down to its bottling strength, usually 80°.

The other method, redistillation, differs only in that the fermented mash is first distilled into a flavorless neutral spirit. Then it is placed in a second still, containing a "gin head", and is redistilled, with vapors absorbing the flavoring agents.

Compound gin, a less costly product, is simply the combination of neutral spirits with the oil and extracts of the botanicals. However, the dominant flavor must be from juniper berries.

4. TEQUILA

The Aztecs did not invent tequila. The one thing that held them back was the failure to discover the secret of distillation. The Aztecs did, however, drink an alcoholic beverage called "Pulque" by the Spaniards. "Pulque" was made by cutting off the flower stalk of the agave plant before it had a chance to bloom, then hollowing out the base of the plant and allowing the cavity to fill with sweet, milky plant sap. With no place to go, the juice would collect there and ferment in a sort of murky, foul-smelling wine.

The Spaniards tried bringing in grapes and grains to recreate alcoholic

beverages popular in Europe, but they wouldn't grow in the semi-arid areas where the agave plant thrived. The Spaniards didn't like the taste of Pulque, so they tried distilling it. After experimenting with different types of agave, they finally produced a drinkable spirit, which they called "Mezcal."

Tequila is not made from cactus. The confusion is common because various agave species are often confused with cacti. Agave leaves are succulent, rather than the stems, as in cactus.

About 125 years ago, several of the distillers around the town of Tequila, in the central Mexican state of Jalisco, began making a superior form of Mezcal. They used the whole heart of a specific variety of agave indigenous to the region: the Blue Agave. Today only spirits made within the confines of this region can bear the name Tequila, with one exception (Chinaco). If produced elsewhere, it must be called Mezcal.

Blue Agave is no longer a wild plant, but has become a carefully cultured species. On average, agave plants are about ten years old before they can be harvested for tequila production.

The juicy core of the plant, which resembles a large pineapple, is harvested. Called the "pina" (Spanish for pineapple), the core, which sometimes weighs upward of 100 pounds is trimmed, cut into chunks, then baked in huge steam ovens. A sweet juice (Aguamiel or honey juice) is extracted by steaming and compressing the pina.

The juice is fermented for several days and then distilled at a low proof. It is then double distilled to a powerful 110 proof. Tequila is reduced to 80 proof with water before bottling.

Some tequila is aged in wood, Gold and "Anejo", and some is bottled clear, the White and Silver.

The Gold tequila rests in large oak vats for about nine months to one year, where it acquires a pale gold color.

By law, tequila, designated "Anejo", must be aged a minimum of one year in wood, however, it is usually aged in smaller oak barrels for at least three years and sometimes up to seven.

There are now premium mezcals made in the manner of tequila but produced outside of the Tequila region. Some mezcal is produced with an agave root worm in the bottle as a mark of authenticity.

6. VODKA

Vodka is far and away the most popular spirit category in America, accounting for more than 20% of all distilled spirits consumption. It is defined by government regulations as a spirit without any distinctive character, aroma, taste or color. Vodka is essentially an unaged neutral spirit that can be distilled from just about anything fermentable. Although the legendary potato is used in the production of some vodkas, most brands today, including the imported ones, are made from grain...any grain, including rye, wheat and barley, but principally corn.

Vodka in most Slavic languages means "water." (Sometimes it's spelled "Woda", but the pronunciation is the same.) The word "vodka" translates literally as "dear little water", an affectionate diminutive for this clean, tasteless spirit that blends with virtually any beverage.

As with Whiskey, the historic origin of vodka remains in question. The Russians and the Poles are just two national groups that claim the distinction of discovering how to produce vodka. There are several others, and as the map of Eastern Europe continues to change, other national groups may lay claim to being the originator of vodka. One thing is certain, however: vodka originated somewhere in Northern and Eastern Europe and several sources

note it's arrival in Russia as early as the 14th century.

Americans knew next to nothing about vodka before the 1930's and what they did know consisted mainly of impressions gleaned from Russian novels and old movies about Czarist Russia. Consumers weren't really aware of vodka until after World War II. Alcohol has always featured large in the lives of the Eastern Europeans. Its influence can be recorded as far back as 988! In that year the Grand Prince of

Kiev was told by his ambassadors that Islam forbade strong drink. Consequently the Prince became a Christian and was sent plentiful supplies of communion wine from Byzantium, which was the seat of orthodox Christianity.

Fermented drink was not enough to satisfy the Eastern Europeans for long. They discovered that the extremes of temperature in that part of the world enabled them to produce a beverage with a higher alcoholic strength.

In the 1540s the Russian tsar Ivan 'the Terrible' established his own network of distilling taverns and ensured that the profits went straight into the imperial treasury. He outlawed taverns that were outside his control and put a ban on distilling by potential rivals. He kept his options open, however! He was always in need of the support of the nobility, so he allowed them to continue distilling vodka.

Restrictions and threats of savage punishment didn't dampen the enthusiasm of people for vodka-making. Secret distilling survived through the next century. At the same time the tsar's taverns flourished and grew in number to such an extent that, by the late seventeenth century, a visitor to Russia remarked that they outnumbered bath-houses.

Successive rulers tightened their monopoly on vodka distilling but continued to curry favor with the nobility, gentry and government officials by granting them distilling rights. Thus, in addition to its social role, vodka had considerable political and economic significance in Russia.

From the beginning of the seventeenth century it had become customary for vodka to be served at Russian imperial banquets. All formal meals began with bread and vodka. Vodka was also drunk ceremoniously at religious festivals and in church ritual, and to refuse to partake could be considered impious.

Peter the Great, tsar of Russia from 1689 to 1721, was renowned for his hospitality and love of drinking. He served large quantities of vodka, his favorite drink, at his legendary banquets. On these occasions he would shock foreign guests by cutting open enormous pies out of which dwarfs would jump.

The Governor of Moscow trained a large bear to serve pepper vodka to his guests. If anyone showed reluctance in accepting the drink, the bear would remove the guest's clothes, an article at a time.

Making vodka was a lot easier in Poland, as fewer official restrictions were imposed. Indeed, in 1546, King Jan Olbrecht issued a decree allowing every citizen the right to make vodka.

As a result many families distilled their own spirit, and as early as the sixteenth century there were forty-nine commercial distilleries in the town of Poznan alone.

Vodka-making and drinking became established at all levels of society in Poland over the next few centuries. Poznan continues to be a major center for the production of vodka today.

The key to distillation is the separation of alcohol from the water content of fermented liquid. Because water freezes at a higher temperature than alcohol, the Eastern Europeans were able to separate the alcohol by freezing fermented liquid during the winter months. As a result they were left with a drink with a higher strength than that produced by fermentation alone. This was the earliest method of producing stronger spirit in Eastern Europe. The techniques of distillation didn't spread from the west until the fifteenth century. From that time to the mid nineteenth century all vodka was made in a pot-still using local natural resources such as wheat, barley, ryes, potatoes and rice.

A mash was created by heating the grain to release the starch for conversion into sugar. The sweet liquid was allowed to ferment naturally before distilling. Gradually vodka-making in Eastern Europe was refined. In the beginning vodka was the product of a single distillation to a relatively low proof, but distillers soon learned the benefits of two or more distillations on product quality.

Extra distillations mean the final spirit has a higher strength and greater purity. Next the Eastern Europeans introduced filtration to improve the purity of the spirit further. This was carried out initially with felt or river sand, but in the late eighteenth century charcoal began to be used. The filtration standards established at that time remain to this day.

With the invention of the continuous still in the last century, distillers were able to produce vodka to a very high proof in a continuous operation.

Most vodka has no color and carries only the clean aroma and character of pure spirit from the still. It has a characteristically light and very slightly oily texture. Different brands have their own characteristics and have been made over the centuries to a variety of styles.

There is a long heritage of making flavored vodkas in Eastern Europe. This goes back to the days of home distillation, when vodka was flavored with herbs, spices and fruit. Nowadays natural flavorings such as cherry, lime, lemon, orange, mint, etc., are added in the final distillation.

HELPFUL HINTS

Cocktail mixing is an art which is expressed in the preparation and presentation of the cocktail.

How to make a Brandy Alexander Cross

Take two short straws and, with a sharp knife, slice one of the straws half way through in the middle and wedge the other uncut straw into the cut straw to create a cross.

Storing Fruit Juices

Take a 750mL/25fl oz bottle and soak it in hot water to remove the label and sterilize the alcohol. The glass has excellent appeal and you'll find it easier to pour the correct measurement with an attached nip pourer.

Sugar Syrup Recipe

Fill a cup or bowl (depending on how much you want to make) with white sugar, top it up with boiling water until the receptacle is just about full and keep stirring until the sugar is fully dissolved. Refrigerate when not in use. Putting a teaspoon of sugar into a cocktail is being lazy, it does not do the job properly as the sugar dissolves.

Juice Tips

Never leave juices, Coconut Cream or other ingredients in cans. Pour them into clean bottles, cap and refrigerate them. All recipes in this book have been tested with Berri fruit juices.

Ice

Ice is probably the most important part of cocktails. It is used in nearly all cocktails. Consequently ice must be clean and fresh at all times.

The small squared cubes and flat chips of ice are superior for chilling and mixing cocktails. Ice cubes with holes are inefficient. Wet ice, ice scraps and broken ice should only be used in blenders.

Crushed Ice

Take the required amount of ice and fold into a clean linen cloth. Although uncivilised, the most effective method is to smash it against the bar floor. Shattering with a bottle may break the bottle. Certain retailers sell portable ice crushers. Alternatively a blender may be used. Half fill with ice and then pour water into the blender until it reaches the level of the ice. Blend for about 30 seconds, strain out the water and you have perfectly crushed ice. Always try and use a metal scoop to collect the ice from the ice tray. Never pick up the ice with your hands. This is unhygienic.

Shovelling the glass into the ice tray to gather ice can also cause breakages and hence should be avoided where possible.

It is important that the ice tray is cleaned each day. As ice is colorless and odorless, many people assume wrongly it is always clean. Taking a cloth soaked in hot water, wipe the inside of the bucket warm. The blenders used for all of our bar requirements are Moulinex blenders with glass bowls. We have found these blenders to be of exceptional quality.

GLASSES

Cordial (Embassy):	30mL	Fancy Hi-Ball Glass:	220mL, 350mL, 470mL
Cordial (Lexington):	37mL	Hurricane Glass:	230mL, 440mL, 650mL
Tall Dutch Cordial:	45mL	Irish Coffee Glass:	250mL
Whisky Shot:	45mL	Margarita Glass:	260mL
Martini Glass:	90mL	Hi-Ball Glass:	270mL, 285mL, 330mL
Cocktail Glass:	90mL, 140mL	Footed Hi-Ball Glass:	270mL, 300mL
Champagne Saucer:	150mL	Salud Grande Glass:	290mL
Champagne Flute:	150mL, 190mL	Fiesta Grande Glass:	350mL, 490mL
Wine Goblet:	140mL, 190mL	Poco Grande Glass:	380mL
Brandy Balloon:	650mL	Fancy Cocktail:	210mL, 300mL

Old Fashioned Spirit: 185mL, 210mL, 290mL

A proven method for cleaning glasses is to hold each glass individually over a bucket of boiling water until the glass becomes steamy and then with a clean linen cloth rub in a circular way to ensure the glass is polished for the next serve. Cocktails can be poured into any glass but the better the glass, the better the appearance of the cocktail. One basic rule should apply and that is: use no colored glasses as they spoil the appearance of cocktails. All glasses have been designed for a specific task, e.g.

1. Hi-Ball glasses for long, cool refreshing drinks.
2. Cocktail glasses for short, sharp, or stronger drinks.
3. Champagne saucers for creamy after-dinner style drinks, etc.

The stem of the glass has been designed so you may hold it whilst polishing, leaving the bowl free of marks and germs so that you may enjoy your drink. All cocktail glasses should be kept in a refrigerator or filled with ice while you are preparing the cocktails in order to chill the glass. An appealing affect on a 90mL cocktail glass can be achieved by running the glass under cold water and then placing it in the freezer.

GARNISHES AND JUICES

Banana

Celery

Cucumber

Lemons

Limes

Mint leaves

Olives

Celery salt

Chocolate flake

Cinnamon

Fresh eggs

Fresh single cream

Fresh milk

Apple

Carbonated waters

Coconut cream

Lemon – pure

Orange

Jelly Babies

Almonds

Apricot conserve

Vanilla ice cream

Onions

Oranges

Pineapple

Red Maraschino Cherries

Rockmelon

Strawberries

Canned fruit

Nutmeg

Pepper, Salt

Tomato

Sugar and sugar cubes

Tabasco sauce

Worcestershire sauce

Orange and Mango

Pineapple

Sugar syrup

Canned nectars

Canned pulps

Crushed pineapple

Blueberries

Red cocktail onions

Flowers (assorted)

Simplicity is the most important fact to keep in mind when garnishing cocktails. Do not overdo the garnish; make it striking, but if you can't get near the cocktail to drink it then you have failed. Most world champion cocktails just have a lemon slice, or a single red cherry.

Tall, refreshing Hi-Balls tend to have more garnish as the glass is larger. A swizzle stick should be served nearly always in long cocktails. Straws are always served for a lady, but optional for a man.

Plastic animals, umbrellas, fans and a whole variety of novelty goods are now available to garnish with, and they add a lot of fun to the drink.

ALCOHOL RECOMMENDED FOR A COCKTAIL BAR

Spirits

Ouzo	Scotch	Bourbon
Southern Comfort	Brandy	Tennessee Whiskey
Campari	Tequila	Canadian Club
Vandermint	Gin	Vodka
Malibu	Pernod	Rum

Liqueurs

Advocaat	Frangelico	Amaretto
Galliano	Baileys Irish Cream	Grand Marnier
Banana	Kahlúa	Benedictine
Kirsch	Blue Curaçao	Kirsch
Cassis	Mango	Chartreuse (both)
Melon	Cherry Advocaat	Orange
Cherry Brandy	Peach	Pimm's
Coconut	Sambucca – Clear	Sambucca – Black
Cointreau	Crème de cafe	Strawberry
Crème de Menthe Green	Triple Sec	Dark Crème de Cacao
Drambuie	Claytons Tonis (non-alcoholic)	

Vermouth

Cinzano Bianco Vermouth	Martini Bianco Vermouth
Cinzano Dry Vermouth	Martini Dry Vermouth
Cinzano Rosso Vermouth	Martini Rosso Vermouth

ESSENTIAL EQUIPMENT FOR A COCKTAIL BAR

Cocktail shaker	Waiter's friend corkscrew
Hawthorn strainer	Bottle openers
Mixing glass	Ice scoop
Spoon with muddler	Ice bucket
Moulinex Electric blender	Free pourers
Knife, cutting board	Swizzle sticks, straws
Measures (jiggers)	Hand cloths for cleaning glasses
Can opener	Scooper spoon (long teaspoon)
Coasters and napkins	

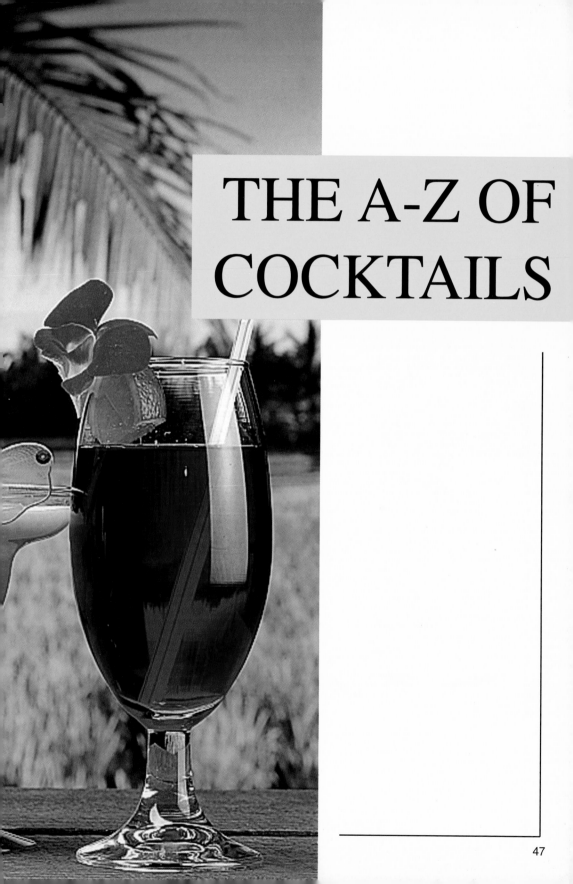

THE A-Z OF COCKTAILS

Scotland

Aberdeen Angus

Ingredients
Glass: 140mL/5fl oz Cocktail Glass
Mixers: 30mL/1fl oz scotch whisky
            10mL/⅜fl oz Drambuie
            1 tablespoon honey
            10mL/⅜fl oz fresh lime juice

Method
Blend with ice and pour.
Garnish with two banana wheel slices
wedged on rim of glass.

Abbey

United Kingdom

Ingredients

Glass: 140mL/5fl oz Cocktail
            Glass
Mixers: 60mL/2fl oz gin
            1 dash sweet vermouth
            30mL/1fl oz orange juice
            1 dash Angostura Bitter

Method
Shake and strain into a glass and
serve. Garnish with Maraschino cherry.

ABC

France

Ingredients

Glass: 185mL/6fl oz Wine Goblet
Mixers: 5 ice cubes
            Champagne or sparkling
            white wine
            20mL/⅜fl oz Armagnac
            20mL/⅜fl oz Benedictine
            1 dash Angostura Bitter

Method
Crack 2 ice cubes and place them into
a shaker with Armagnac, Benedictine
and Angostura Bitter and shake well.
Crush remaining ice cubes and empty
into a goblet. Drain contents of shaker
of the crushed ice and top with
champagne. Serve garnished with
lemon slice, orange segments and
cherries.

Sweden

Absolut Cosmopolitan

Ingredients

Glass: 90mL/3oz Martini Glass
Mixers: 45mL/1½fl oz Absolut Citron
20mL/⅝fl oz Triple Sec
20mL/⅝fl oz cranberry juice
juice of ½ fresh lime

Method

Shake with ice and strain into chilled martini glass.
Garnish with an orange twist.

Abortion

Australia

Ingredients

Glass: 90mL/3 oz Cocktail Glass
Mixers: 30 mL/1 oz vodka
30 mL/1 oz Sambucca
30 mL/1 oz Baileys Irish Cream
3 drops Grenadine

Method

Layer into cocktail glass and serve.

Absinth

France

Ingredients

Glass: 90mL/3 oz Cocktail Glass
Mixers: 50mL/1¾fl oz Pernod
1 teaspoon anisette
2 tablespoon water
1 dash orange bitters

Method

Shake ingredients with ice and strain into a chilled cocktail glass.

Mexico

Acapulco

Ingredients

Glass: 150mL/5fl oz Old Fashioned
Glass
Mixers: 30mL/1fl oz Bacardi
10mL/1fl oz Cointreau
1 egg white
15mL/⅜fl oz fresh lime juice
add sugar to taste

Method
Shake over ice and pour. Garnish with
partially torn mint leaves.

Acapulco I

Mexico

Ingredients

Glass: 285mL/9½fl oz Cocktail
Glass
Mixers: 30mL/1fl oz tequila
30mL/1fl oz dark rum
30mL/1fl oz Tia Maria
150mL/5fl oz coconut
cream

Method
Shake ingredients and strain over ice
into a cocktail glass and serve.

Admiral Cannon

U.S.A.

Ingredients

Glass: 140mL/5oz Cocktail
Glass
Mixers: 45mL/1½fl oz bourbon
15mL/½fl oz lemon juice
30mL/1fl oz white rum
1 teaspoon maple syrup

Method
Shake and strain into cocktail glass
over cracked ice and serve.

African Nipple

South Africa

Ingredients

Glass: 140mL/5oz Champagne Saucer
Mixers: 30 mL/1fl oz vodka
1 tsp Grenadine
30 mL/1fl oz Afrikoko
60 mL/2fl oz cream

Method

Shake and strain into a champagne saucer and serve.

After Eight

Australia

Ingredients

Glass: Tall Dutch Cordial
Mixers: 15mL/½fl oz Kahlúa
20 mL/¾fl oz Baileys Irish Cream
10 mL/⅜fl oz Crème de Menthe

Method

Layer ingredients in order into a tall Dutch cordial glass or shot glass and serve.

U.S.A.

Alabama Slammer

Ingredients

Glass: Whisky Shot
Mixers: 10 mL/⅜fl oz gin
10 mL/⅜fl oz Amaretto
10 mL/⅜fl oz orange juice
10 mL/½fl oz Southern Comfort

Method

Pour in order then shoot.
A real drink! From the heart of the Deep South, USA.

Alaska

Ingredients

Glass: 130mL/4½oz Cocktail Glass

Mixers: 30mL/1fl oz gin
10mL/⅜fl oz Yellow Chartreuse
1-2 dashes of Orange Curaçao

Method

Shake over ice and strain. Garnish with orange twist.

Alexander

United Kingdom

Ingredients

Glass: 90mL/3 oz Cocktail Glass

Mixers: 45mL/1½fl oz gin
20mL/⅝ ₂fl oz Crème de Cacao
nutmeg
15mL/½fl oz fresh cream

Method

Shake liquid ingredients and strain into cocktail glass. Cross two straws over glass, sprinkle nutmeg over the top. Remove straws and serve.

Alfonso

France

Ingredients

Glass: 90mL/3 oz Cocktail Glass

Mixers: 15mL/½fl oz dry gin
4 dashes sweet vermouth
15mL/½fl oz French vermouth
1 dash Angostura Bitter
30 mL/1 oz Grand Marnier
4 ice cubes

Method

Shake and strain into a 3 oz cocktail glass and serve.

Alice in Wonderland

Morocco

Ingredients
Glass: 170mL/6oz Champagne flute
Mixers: 100mL/3⅜fl oz grapefruit juice
30mL/1fl oz green tea
20mL/⅝fl oz lemon juice
15mL/½fl oz sugar syrup
top up with soda

Method
Build over ice and top up with soda.
Garnish with white grapes.

Alice

Germany

Ingredients
Glass: 140mL/5oz Champagne
flute
Mixers: 30mL/1 oz scotch whiskey
30mL/1 oz kümmel liqueur
30mL/1 oz sweet
vermouth

Method
Half fill mixing glass with ice and add
liquid ingredients. Stir and strain into 5
oz champagne glass. Garnish with
lemon peel and serve.

All Night

Mexico

Ingredients
Glass: 90mL/3oz Cocktail Glass
Mixers: 30mL/1fl oz tequila
1 dash Grenadine
20mL/⅝fl oz lime juice
1 egg white

Method
Shake ingredients and strain into
cocktail glass. Garnish with
Maraschino cherry and serve.

Belgium

Almond Orange frost

Ingredients
Glass: 240mL/8oz Champagne
           Sherbert Glass
Mixers: 15mL/½fl oz Amaretto
           15mL/½fl oz Frangelico
           15mL/½fl oz Chambord
           10mL/⅜fl oz fresh lime juice
           10mL/⅜fl oz fresh lemon juice
           1 teaspoon chopped almonds
           2 scoops orange sherbert

Method
Blend with ice. Garnish with orange slice
and chopped almonds.

Almond Joy

Italy

Ingredients

Glass: 300mL/10oz Tulip Glass
Mixers: 30mL/1fl oz Amaretto
           90mL/3fl oz milk
           1 dash Crème de Cacao
           30mL/1fl oz coconut syrup
           1 scoop ice cream

Method
Blend ingredients and pour into tulip
glass, garnish with a pineapple wedge,
straws and serve.

Altered States Shooter

U.S.A.

Ingredients

Glass: Whiskey shot
Mixers: banana
           15mL/½fl oz Kahlúa
           15mL/½fl oz peach liqueur
           15mL/½fl oz Baileys Irish
           Cream

Method
Layer in a shot glass and serve.

Philippines

Amaretto Choco Cream

Ingredients

Glass: 240mL/8oz Champagne
           Sherbert Glass
Mixers: 30mL/1fl oz Amaretto
           30mL/1fl oz Kahlúa
           30mL/1fl oz Chocolate Syrup
           2 scoops of vanilla ice cream

Method

Blend without ice and pour over ice.
Garnish with aerosol whipping cream.
Comments: Filipinos love their ice cream
and adopted this innovative recipe to
include one of their favourite desserts.

Amaretto Sour

Italy

Ingredients

Glass: 140mL/5oz Wine Glass
Mixers: 45mL/1½fl oz Amaretto
         ½ lemon, squeezed
         soda water

Method

Shake Amaretto, lemon juice and ice,
pour into a wine glass and top with
soda. Garnish with a strip of lemon
peel and serve.

Amaretto Stinger

U.S.A.

Ingredients

Glass: 90mL/3oz Cocktail
           Glass
Mixers: 45mL/1½fl oz Amaretto
         3 ice cubes
         30mL/1fl oz white Crème de
         Menthe

Method

Shake well, strain into cocktail glass
and serve.

Americano

Italy

Ingredients
Glass: 270mL/9oz Hi-Ball Glass
Mixers: 30mL/1fl oz campari
30mL/1fl oz Cinzano Rosso Vermouth
top up with soda

Method
Build over ice and top up with soda.
Garnish with orange slice.
Comments: originated from European travellers visiting America desiring a taste of European aperitifs.

American Beauty

U.S.A.

Ingredients
Glass: 140mL/5oz Cocktail Glass
Mixers: 15mL/½fl oz brandy
15mL/½fl oz Grenadine
15mL/½fl oz dry vermouth
15mL/½fl oz orange juice
port wine
3 dashes white Crème de Menthe

Method
Shake all ingredients except port wine.
Strain into a 5oz glass, top with port wine and serve.

Amsterdam

Netherlands

Ingredients
Glass: 90mL/3oz Cocktail Glass
Mixers: 30mL/1fl oz gin
4 dashes orange bitters
15mL/½fl oz orange juice
15mL/½fl oz Cointreau
cracked ice

Method
Shake ingredients and strain cocktail glass and serve.

Anabolic Steroid

Australia

Ingredients

Glass: Tall Dutch Cordial
Mixers: 15mL/½fl oz Midori
15mL/½fl oz Cointreau
15mL/½fl oz Blue Curaçao

Method
Layer in a shot glass and serve.

Angel Dew

Switzerland

Ingredients

Glass: Cordial (Embassy)
Mixers: 15mL/½fl oz Benedictine
15mL/½fl oz Baileys Irish
Cream

Method
Layer in a shot glass and serve.

U.S.A.

Andy Williams

Ingredients
Glass: 290mL/10oz Old Fashioned
Spirit Glass
Mixers: 60mL/2fl oz Clayton's Tonic
15mL/½fl oz lime juice
dash sugar syrup
top up with soda water

Method
Shake with ice and pour. Garnish with a
thin lime slice floated in the drink.
Comments: a delightful predinner drink.

Angel's Kiss

Brazil

Ingredients
Glass: 290mL/9oz Poco Grande
Glass
Mixers: scoop vanilla ice cream
1 tablespoon passionfruit pulp
150mL/5fl oz Apricot nectar

Method
Blend with ice and pour. Garnish with mint leaves.
A wonderful blend of passionfruit and apricots.

Angelique

France

Ingredients

Glass: 140mL/5oz Champagne
Saucer
Mixers: 30mL/1fl oz ouzo
30mL/1fl oz fresh cream
30mL/1fl oz Advocaat
30mL/1fl oz orange juice
30mL/1fl oz Strega

Method
Shake and strain into a champagne saucer. Garnish with Maraschino cherry and serve.

Angry Fijian

Fiji

Ingredients

Glass: 90mL/3oz Cocktail Glass
Mixers: 30mL/1fl oz banana liqueur
30mL/1fl oz Baileys Irish
Cream
30mL/1fl oz Malibu

Method
Layer in a 3 oz cocktail glass and serve.

U.S.A.

Apple Buck

Ingredients

Glass: 270mL/9oz Footed Hi-Ball
Glass

Mixers: 30mL/1fl oz apple brandy
10mL/⅜fl oz brandy
10mL/⅜fl oz lemon juice
2 slices of fresh ginger
top up with ginger ale

Method

Shake over ice and pour, then top with ginger ale. Garnish with apple peel.

Appease Me

Australia

Ingredients

Glass: 270mL/9oz Hi-Ball Glass
Mixers: 30mL/1fl oz mango liqueur
60mL/2fl oz orange juice
30mL/1fl oz Advocaat
30mL/1fl oz cream
30mL/1fl oz vodka
2 slices mango

Method

Blend ingredients with ice and pour into a 10oz hi-ball glass. Garnish with the pulp of half a passionfruit and serve with straws.

Apple Magic

U.S.A.

Ingredients

Glass: 270mL/9oz Hi-Ball Glass
Mixers: 30mL/1fl oz Midori
15mL/½fl oz orange juice
15mL/½fl oz Southern
Comfort
90mL/3fl oz apple juice
15mL/½fl oz Grand Marnier
ice

Method

Blend and pour into a colada glass. Garnish with a slice of apple and strawberry and serve.

Apres Ski

Canada

Ingredients

Glass: 270mL/9oz Hi-Ball Glass
Mixers: 30mL/1fl oz Crème de
           Menthe
           15mL/½fl oz Pernod
           15mL/½fl oz vodka
           lemonade

Method

Third fill a 10 oz hi-ball glass with ice
and pour ingredients over ice. Top with
lemonade and serve with straws.

Apricot Smoothie

U.S.A.

Ingredients

Glass: 390mL/12oz Poco Grande
           Glass
Mixers: 2 apricots
           90mL/3fl oz milk
           15mL/½fl oz lemon juice
           30mL/1fl oz vanilla yoghurt

Method

Blend with ice and pour.
Garnish with apricot slice and straws.

Aqua Thunder

Cuba

Ingredients

Glass: 270mL/9oz Hi-Ball Glass
Mixers: 10mL/⅜fl oz Blue Curaçao
           10mL/⅜fl oz banana liqueur
           30mL/1fl oz melon liqueur
           10mL/⅜fl oz freshly squeezed
           lemon
           top-up with soda water

Method

Build over ice. Garnish with swizzle stick
and slice of lemon.
Comments: watch in wonder as the soda
waterfall splashes over the ice creating a
thunderous aqua-colored spectacular.

Aquavit fiz

Denmark

Ingredients
Glass: 170mL/6oz Tulip Champagne
          Glass
Mixers: 45mL/1½fl oz Aquavit
          30mL/1fl oz lemon juice
          15mL/½fl oz Cherry Heering
          10mL/⅜fl oz sugar syrup
          1 egg white
          top up with soda

Method
Shake over ice and strain then top up with
soda. Garnish with a red cherry.

Argyle Tavern

Australia

Ingredients
Glass: 150mL/5oz Cocktail Glass
Mixers: 60mL/2fl oz brandy
          15mL/½fl oz almond liqueur
          15mL/½fl oz Galliano
          30mL/1fl oz dry vermouth

Method
Half fill a mixing glass with cracked ice
and add ingredients. Stir and strain into
cocktail glass, garnish with Maraschino
cherry and serve.

Aspiration

New Zealand

Ingredients
Glass: 150mL/5oz Cocktail Glass
Mixers: 30mL/1fl oz Midori
          30mL/1fl oz pineapple juice
          15mL/½fl oz Galliano
          1 kiwifruit
          10mL/⅜fl oz white curaçao
          1 dash coconut cream

Method
Blend and pour into a colada glass.
Garnish with a slice of kiwifruit
and serve.

Atomic Bomb

China

Ingredients

Glass: Tall Dutch Cordial
Mixers: 20mL/⅝fl oz Tia Maria
15mL/½fl oz gin
10mL/⅜fl oz cream

Method
Layer in order, then float cream.

Astronaut

U.S.A.

Ingredients

Glass: 90mL/3oz Cocktail Glass
Mixers: 30mL/1fl oz dark rum
30mL/1fl oz vodka
15mL/½fl oz fresh lemon
juice
6 drops of passionfruit pulp

Method
Shake over ice and strain. Garnish with ½ scoop of passionfruit.

Aussie Slinger

Australia

Ingredients

Glass: 270mL/9oz Hi-Ball Glass
Mixers: 45mL/1½fl oz any white
spirit
lemonade
30mL/1fl oz Grenadine
1 dash Angostura Bitter
60mL/2fl oz lemon juice
1 cracked ice

Method
Half fill hi-ball glass with cracked ice, add ingredients and top with lemonade. Garnish with ½ orange slice, ½ lemon slice, 1 Maraschino cherry, swizzle stick, straws and serve.

Australia

Australian Gold

Ingredients
Glass: 90mL/3oz Cocktail Glass
Mixers: 30mL/1fl oz dark rum
           30mL/1fl oz mango liqueur
           30mL/1fl oz Galliano

Method
Build over ice.

Autumn Leaf

Sweden

Ingredients
Glass: 90mL/3oz Cocktail Glass
Mixers: 30mL/1fl oz Arrak
           30mL/1fl oz Dazzinger
           goldwasser
           30mL/1fl oz Crème de
           Cacao

Method
Mix in mixing glass with cracked ice,
strain into cocktail glass and serve.

Avalanche

U.S.A.

Ingredients
Glass: 140mL/5oz Champagne
           Flute
Mixers: 30mL/1fl oz Cointreau
           30mL/1fl oz orange juice
           30mL/1fl oz Tia Maria
           60mL/2fl oz cream

Method
Shake and strain into a
champagne glass and serve.

Italy

B & B

Ingredients
Glass: Brandy Balloon
Mixers: 30mL/1fl oz Cognac
30mL/1fl oz Benedictine

Method
Build, no ice.
Tempt your pallet with this historical blend of choice liqueurs. Relaxing by the fire on winter nights, the genuine connoisseur will enjoy interesting conversation with friends. Ideal with coffee.

B & G

France

Ingredients
Glass: 180mL/6oz Old Fashioned Glass
Mixers: 30mL/1fl oz Benedictine
30mL/1fl oz Grand Mariner

Method
Pour over ice in an old fashioned glass.

B & P

Spain

Ingredients
Glass: Brandy Balloon
Mixers: 30mL/1fl oz Benedictine
60mL/2fl oz port wine

Method
Pour over ice in a brandy balloon and serve.

Bacardi Blossom

Cuba

Ingredients

Glass: 90mL/3oz Cocktail Glass
Mixers: 45mL/1½fl oz Bacardi rum
10mL/⅜fl oz orange juice
10mL/⅜fl oz lemon juice
1 teaspoon sugar

Method
Shake and strain into cocktail glass
and serve.

Bacardi No. 2

U.S.A.

Ingredients

Glass: 140mL/5oz Cocktail Glass
Mixers: 60mL/1fl oz Bacardi rum
1 egg white
dash of Grenadine
ice
20mL/⅝fl oz lemon or lime
juice

Method
Shake and strain into cocktail glass
and serve.

United Kingdom

Badminton

Ingredients
Glass: 250mL/8oz Red Wine Goblet
Mixers: 120mL/4fl oz red wine
1 teaspoon sugar
sprinkle of nutmeg
top up with soda

Method
Stir sugar in red wine and add nutmeg
then top up with soda. Garnish with a
cucumber slice.

Bahama Mama

Ingredients

The Bahamas

Glass: 285mL/9½oz Hi-Ball Glass
Mixers: 15mL/½fl oz Bacardi Gold
Rum
15mL/½fl oz Malibu
15mL/½fl oz Banana
Liqueur
15mL/½fl oz Grenadine
90mL/3fl oz orange juice
60mL/2fl oz pineapple juice

Method
Blend over ice. Garnish with a
pineapple wedge and leaves.

Baileys Coconut Cream

Ingredients

Trinidad

Glass: 150mL/5oz Wine Glass
Mixers: 30mL/1fl oz Baileys Irish
Cream
30mL/1fl oz cream
15mL/½fl oz Malibu
60mL/2fl oz orange juice

Method
Shake ingredients and pour over
cracked ice in wine glass. Add a dash
of Grenadine and serve with straws.

Ballet Russe

Russia

Ingredients
Glass: 150mL/5oz Old Fashioned
Spirit Glass
Mixers: 30mL/1fl oz vodka
15mL/½fl oz Crême de Cassis
15mL/½fl oz fresh lime juice
15mL/½fl oz fresh lemon juice

Method
Shake with ice and strain. Garnish with an
orange slice and a red cherry.

U.S.A.

Baltimore Zoo

Ingredients
Glass: 300mL/10oz Footed Pilsener Glass
Mixers: 15mL/½fl oz dark rum
15mL/½fl oz gin
15mL/½fl oz Cointreau
60mL/2fl oz cranberry juice
top with draft beer

Method
Shake with ice and strain then top with draft beer.

Bamboo

Spain

Ingredients
Glass: 150mL/5fl oz Cocktail Glass
Mixers: 30mL/1fl oz dry vermouth
30mL/1fl oz dry sherry
1 dash orange bitters
2 dashes Angostura Bitter

Method
Mix ingredients in a mixing glass, strain into cocktail glass. Garnish with Maraschino cherry and serve.

Banana Bender

Australia

Ingredients
Glass: 150mL/5oz Champagne Flute
Mixers: 30mL/1fl oz Cointreau
60mL/2fl oz cream
30mL/1fl oz banana liqueur
½ banana

Method
Blend ingredients until smooth, pour into champagne glass and serve.

Banana Bliss

Japan

Ingredients

Glass: 180mL/6oz Old Fashioned
         Glass
Mixers: 30mL/1fl oz cognac
         crushed ice
         30mL/1fl oz banana liqueur

Method
Fill a 6 oz old fashioned glass
with crushed ice, build liquid
ingredients and serve.

Banana-Choc Shake

U.S.A.

Ingredients

Glass: 440mL/14oz Hurricane
         Glass
Mixers: 1 ripe banana, sliced
         2 scoops chocolate ice
         cream
         210mL/7fl oz milk

Method
Blend with ice and pour.
Garnish with teaspoon of grated
chocolate and straw.

Banana Colada

U.S.A.

Ingredients
Glass: 300mL/10oz Fancy Glass
Mixers: 30mL/1fl oz Bacardi
         30mL/1fl oz sugar syrup
         30mL/1fl oz coconut cream
         30mL/1fl oz cream
         120mL/4fl oz pineapple juice
         ½ banana

Method
Blend with ice and pour.
Garnish: slice of banana, pineapple spear
and mint leaves. Serves with straws.

Cuba

Banana Daiquiri

Ingredients
Glass: 140mL/5oz Champagne
          Saucer
Mixers: 1 banana
          15mL/½fl oz sugar syrup
          30mL/1fl oz Bacardi
          45mL/1½fl oz lemon juice
          30mL/1fl oz banana liqueur

Method
Blend with ice and strain.
Garnish with a round slice of
banana and mint leaves.

Banana Jaffa

Portugal

Ingredients

Glass: 270mL/9oz Hi-Ball Glass
Mixers: 15mL/½fl oz Kahlúa
          30mL/1fl oz cream
          15mL/½fl oz brandy
          ½ banana
          30mL/1fl oz orange juice

Method
Blend until smooth, pour into hi-ball
glass. Garnish with an orange wheel.
pineapple wedge, straws and serve.

Banana Margarita

Mexico

Ingredients

Glass: 150mL/5oz Margarita Glass
Mixers: 30mL/1fl oz tequila
          30mL/1fl oz lemon juice
          15mL/½fl oz Cointreau
          ½ small banana
          15mL/½fl oz banana liqueur
          cracked ice

Method
Blend until smooth, pour into a salt
rimmed margarita glass and serve.

Bananarama

Australia

Ingredients

Glass: 140mL/5oz Cocktail Glass
Mixers: 30mL/1fl oz vodka
30mL/1fl oz Kahlúa
15mL/½fl oz Baileys Irish
Cream
1 banana
60mL/2fl oz cream

Method

Blend with ice and pour.
Garnish with two banana wheel slices
wedged on rim of glass.

Banger

U.S.A.

Ingredients

Glass: 300mL/10oz Hi-Ball Glass
Mixers: 30mL/1fl oz Bacardi rum
180mL/6fl oz orange juice
15mL/½fl oz Galliano
cracked ice

Method

Build over cracked ice in hi-ball
glass. Garnish with orange wheel,
straws and serve.

Bango

Barbados

Ingredients

Glass: 170mL/6oz Tulip
Champagne Glass
Mixers: 45mL/1½fl oz mango
liqueur
slice of pineapple
15mL/½fl oz Malibu
60mL/2fl oz pineapple juice

Method

Blend until smooth, pour into a flute
glass and serve.

Banshee

Antigua

Ingredients

Glass: Brandy Balloon
Mixers: 30mL/1fl oz rum
60mL/2fl oz cream
20mL/⅝fl oz Crème de
Cacao
1 banana
15mL/½fl oz banana
liqueur

Method

Blend until smooth, pour into a brandy
balloon and serve.

Banshee No. 2

Antigua

Ingredients

Glass: 150mL/5oz Cocktail Glass
Mixers: 30mL/1fl oz banana liqueur
60mL/2fl oz cream
30mL/1fl oz white Crème de
Cacao
ice

Method

Shake and strain into cocktail glass.
Garnish with a cherry and serve.

Scotland

Barley Punch

Ingredients

Glass: 210mL/7oz Fancy Hi-Ball
Glass
Mixers: 60mL/2oz ground barley
30mL/1oz sugar
top up with boiling water
peel of 1 lime

Method

Build and top up with boiling water.
Refrigerate until ready to serve. Garnish
with lime peel.

Bee Sting

United Arab Emirates

Ingredients

Glass: Cordial (Lexington)
Mixers: 20mL/⅝fl oz tequila
           10mL/⅜fl oz yellow
           Chartreuse

Method

Layer in order in a shot glass, ignite
and serve.

Bellini

Italy

Ingredients

Glass: 140mL/5oz Champagne
           Flute
Mixers: 45mL/1½fl oz peach juice
           Champagne (chilled)

Method

Place peach juice in a tulip flute, top
with champagne and serve.

Bellini (frozen)

Italy

Ingredients

Glass: 140mL/5oz Champagne
           Flute
Mixers: 60mL/2fl oz peach slices with
           syrup
           30mL/1fl oz vodka
           30mL/1fl oz peach liqueur
           1 teaspoon sugar
           top up with Champagne

Method

Blend with ice, strain and top up with
champagne.

Australia

Blueberry Delight

Ingredients
Glass: 140mL/5oz Cocktail Glass
Mixers: 30mL/1fl oz black Sambucca
           20mL/⅝fl oz coconut liqueur
           10mL/⅜fl oz strawberry liqueur
           60mL/2fl oz cream

Method
Shake with ice and strain.
Garnish with strawberry on side of glass
with blueberries on a toothpick.

Blueberry Delight No. 2

Italy

Ingredients
Glass: 300mL/10oz Hi-Ball Glass
Mixers: 15mL/½fl oz Galleon
           Liverno
           15mL/½fl oz Blue Curaçao
           15mL/½fl oz dry vermouth

Method
Shake ingredients except lemonade
and strain into hi-ball glass. Top with
lemonade, garnish with an lemon
wheel, mint leaves, straws and serve.

Blue Blazer

Scotland

Ingredients
Glass: 140mL Champagne
           Saucer
Mixers: 60mL/1fl oz Scotch
           whiskey
           60mL/1fl oz boiling water
           2 Mugs (silver or copper)
           sugar

Method
Pour whiskey into one mug and water
into the other. Ignite whiskey and pour
into water mug. Pour ingredients from
one mug to the other a few times. Add
sugar to taste, garnish with lemon peel
and serve.

Blue Day

Poland

Ingredients

Glass: 90mL/3oz Cocktail Glass
Mixers: 45mL/1½fl oz vodka
20mL/⅝fl oz Blue Curaçao
peel ½ lemon

Method

Crack ice and place in shaker with liquid ingredients, shake and strain into cocktail glass. Squeeze ½ lemon peel over the top, garnish with the lemon slice and serve.

Blue Dove

U.S.A.

Ingredients

Glass: 300mL/10oz Hi-Ball Glass
Mixers: 30mL/1fl oz Blue Curaçao
lemonade
20mL/⅝fl oz vodka
whipped cream

Method

Pour Blue Curaçao and vodka over ice in hi-ball glass. Top with lemonade, add whipped cream to top and serve.

Blue French

France

Ingredients

Glass: 285mL/10oz Hi-Ball Glass
Mixers: 30mL/1fl oz Pernod
5mL/⅛fl oz Blue Curaçao liqueur
5mL/⅛fl oz lemon juice
top-up with bitter lemon

Method

Build over ice and stir.
Garnish with lemon slice on side of glass, swizzle stick and straws.
A great thirst quencher. Ideal when relaxing by the pool.

Bosom Caresser

Ingredients
Glass: 140mL/5oz Champagne
Saucer
Mixers: 30mL/1fl oz brandy
15mL/½fl oz orange liqueur
5mL/⅛fl oz Grenadine
cordial
1 egg yolk

Method
Shake with ice and strain.
Garnish with two red cherries, slit on side
of glass.
Close to every lady's heart! Egg yolk
allows the cocktail to breathe supporting
the brandy's body and bounce. Fine on
any occasion.

Bosom Caresser No. 2

Ingredients
Glass: 90mL/3oz Cocktail Glass
Mixers: 45mL/1½fl oz brandy
1 egg yolk
15mL/½fl oz Blue Curaçao
1 teaspoon Grenadine

Method
Shake and strain into cocktail glass
and serve.

Bossa Nova

Ingredients
Glass: 285mL/9½oz Footed Hi-Ball
Glass
Mixers: 30mL/1 oz Galleon Liverno
60mL/1 oz pineapple juice
30mL/1 oz light dark rum
10mL/⅜fl oz lemon juice
10mL/⅜fl oz apricot brandy
15mL/½fl oz egg white

Method
Shake and pour over ice in a hi-ball
glass. Garnish with fruit and serve.

Boston Cream

U.S.A.

Ingredients
Glass: 120mL/4oz Cocktail Glass, Frosted
Mixers: 30mL/1fl oz cream
15mL/½fl oz lime juice
30mL/1fl oz coconut cream
15mL/½fl oz Grenadine

Method
Shake over ice and strain. Garnish with a chocolate cross.

Boston Cocktail

U.S.A.

Ingredients

Glass: 90mL/3oz Cocktail Glass
Mixers: 30mL/1fl oz gin
30mL/1fl oz apricot brandy
5mL/⅛fl oz lemon juice
5mL/⅛fl oz Grenadine

Method
Shake over ice and strain then add Grenadine. Garnish with a red cherry.

Bourbon Banana

U.S.A.

Ingredients

Glass: Brandy Balloon
Mixers: 30mL/1fl bourbon
30mL/1fl orange juice
30mL/1fl Kahlúa
30mL/1fl cream
1 banana

Method
Blend ingredients with ice and serve in a brandy balloon.

Brain Dead

U.S.A.

Ingredients

Glass: Whiskey Shot
Mixers: 10mL/⅜fl oz Southern
Comfort
10mL/⅜fl oz tequila
10mL/⅜fl oz Galliano
10mL/⅜fl oz Tia Maria
10mL/⅜fl oz Blue Curaçao

Method
Layer in a test tube or shot glass and
serve.

Brandy Boss

Netherlands

Ingredients

Glass: 140mL/5oz Champagne
Saucer
Mixers: 30mL/1fl oz brandy
15mL/½fl oz Tia Maria
15mL/½fl oz Vandermint
60mL/2fl oz cream

Method
Shake and strain into a champagne
saucer and serve.

Brandy Alexander

United Kingdom

Ingredients
Glass: 140mL/5oz Champagne
Saucer
Mixers: 30mL/1fl oz Brandy
30mL/1fl oz Dark Crème de
Cacao Liqueur
5mL/⅛fl oz Grenadine cordial
30mL/1fl oz cream

Method
Shake with ice and strain.
Garnish with a sprinkle of nutmeg and a
cherry.
An after-dinner cocktail. An "Alexander"
replaces the cacao with green Crème de
Menthe. Cognac may be substituted for
brandy to deliver an exceptional after
taste.

Brandy Daisy

France

Ingredients

Glass: 285mL/9½oz Wine Goblet
Mixers: 60 mL/2fl oz brandy
6 dashes Grenadine
30mL/1fl oz lemon juice
soda water
cracked ice

Method

Fill a goblet with cracked ice, shake brandy, lemon juice and Grenadine. Strain into goblet, top soda. Garnish with mint leaves and orange slice.

Brandy Egg Nog

U.S.A.

Ingredients

Glass: 300mL/10oz Hi-Ball Glass
Mixers: 30mL/1fl oz brandy
1 egg yolk
5mL/⅛fl oz sugar syrup
milk

Method

Shake all ingredients except milk, strain into hi-ball glass. Top with milk, sprinkle with nutmeg, add straws and serve.

Brandy Ice

Portugal

Ingredients

Glass: 285mL/9½oz Tall Wine Glass
Mixers: 30mL/1fl oz brandy
15mL/½fl oz vanilla extract
2 scoops vanilla ice cream
15mL/½fl oz lemon juice
top up with bitter lemon

Method

Blend with ice and strain then top up with bitter lemon. Garnish with an orange slice and a cherry.

Brandy Snaps

Ingredients
Glass: Cordial (Embassy)
Mixers: 10mL/⅜fl oz brandy
          10mL/⅜fl oz peach schnapps
          10mL/⅜fl oz apple juice

Method
Layer brandy onto peach schnapps, then pour apple juice. Garnish with floated cream (optional).

Brandy Riviera

France

Ingredients
Glass: 140mL/5oz Champagne
          Saucer
Mixers: 30mL/1fl oz brandy
          30mL/1fl oz Vandermint
          30mL/1fl oz banana liqueur

Method
Pour ingredients over ice in a champagne saucer and serve.

Brandy Toddy

Wales

Ingredients
Glass: 140mL/3oz Cocktail Glass
Mixers: 60mL/2fl oz brandy
          1 teaspoon sugar
          water
          cracked ice

Method
Dissolve sugar in a little water in the cocktail glass. Add ice, brandy and serve.

Brazil

Brazilian Monk

Ingredients
Glass: 285mL/9⅛oz Tulip Wine Glass
Mixers: 30mL/1fl oz Kahlúa
           15mL/½fl oz Frangelico
           15mL/½fl oz dark Crème de
           Cacao
           2 scoops vanilla ice cream

Method
Blend with ice. Garnish with a wild flower or flower petals.
Very popular in the South American countries and the United States.
Frangelico is imported from Italy and made from wild flowers infused into hazelnuts.

Brazilian Breakdance

Break Shooter

Brazil

Australia

Ingredients
Glass: 390mL/12oz Poco Grande
           Glass
Mixers: 2 teaspoons instant coffee
           scoop vanilla ice cream
           125mL/4fl oz Milk

Method
Blend with ice and pour.
Garnish with a teaspoon chocolate flakes.
A luscious, thick glass of iced coffee flavor, with just a hint of sweetness.

Ingredients
Glass: Cordial (Lexington)
Mixers: 10 mL Kahlúa
           10mL/⅜fl oz ouzo
           10mL/⅜fl oz banana liqueur

Method
Layer in order in a shot glass and serve.

Brittany

France

Ingredients

Glass: 150mL/5oz Old Fashioned Spirit Glass

Mixers: 30mL/1fl oz gin
15mL/½fl oz Amer Picon
10mL/⅜fl oz orange juice
10mL/⅜fl oz lemon juice

Method

Blend with ice and pour.
Garnish with two banana wheel slices wedged on rim of glass.

Bronx

U.S.A.

Ingredients

Glass: 90mL/3oz Cocktail Glass

Mixers: 30mL/1fl oz gin
15mL/½fl oz orange juice
1 dash French vermouth
cracked ice
1 dash Italian vermouth

Method

Shake and strain into 3 oz cocktail glass and serve.

Brown Betty

United Kingdom

Ingredients

Glass: Brandy Balloon

Mixers: 60mL/2fl oz beer or ale
1 tablespoon brown sugar
15mL/½fl oz brandy
1 pinch cinnamon
30mL/1fl oz water
nutmeg
pinch ground cloves
½ slice toasted bread
½ fresh ginger root

Method

Dissolve sugar in water and allow to stand for 15 minutes. Add cloves, brandy and beer or ale and stir well. Pour into brandy balloon, break toasted bread into it. Sprinkle with nutmeg and grate ginger root over top and serve.

Café Nero

Italy

Ingredients
Glass: 140mL/5oz Champagne
               Saucer
Mixers: 30mL/1fl oz Galliano
               black coffee
               fresh cream
               sugar

Method
Firstly, sprinkle white sugar inside the glass after coating with Galliano. Set Galliano alight and twirl the glass so that flames burn brightly. Pour black coffee gently into glass then layer cream on top of the burning coffee. Sprinkle grated chocolate over the coffee.

Café Paris

France

Ingredients

Glass: 140mL/5oz Cocktail Glass
Mixers: 60 mL/2fl oz gin
              10mL/⅜fl oz double cream
              5mL/⅛fl oz Pernod
              1 egg white

Method
Shake over ice and strain. Garnish with half a slice of lemon.

Café Royal

France

Ingredients

Glass: Irish Coffee Glass
Mixers: black coffee
              1 lump sugar
              30mL/1fl oz brandy

Method
Place sugar in spoon and hold over coffee, fill spoon with brandy and ignite. When flame starts to fade place spoon in coffee and serve.

Cameron Cannon

U.S.A.

Ingredients

Glass: 150mL/5oz Cocktail Glass
Mixers: 30mL/1fl oz Kahlúa
30mL/1fl oz Baileys Irish
Cream
90mL/3fl oz vodka
dash Crème de Menthe
3 drops green Chartreuse

Method

Shake and strain into cocktail glass
and serve.

Campino

Italy

Ingredients

Glass: 210mL/7oz Old Fashioned
Mixers: 15mL/½fl oz Campari
2 dashes Crème de Cassis
15mL/½fl oz sweet
vermouth
15mL/½fl oz dry vermouth
soda water
15mL/½fl oz gin

Method

Mix all ingredients except soda water
and peel in mixing glass. Pour into
tumbler and top with soda. Garnish
with orange peel and serve.

Canadian Daisy

Canada

Ingredients

Glass: 285mL/9½oz Hi-Ball Glass
Mixers: 30mL/1fl oz Canadian Club
Whisky
10mL/⅜fl oz brandy
10mL/⅜fl oz lemon juice
5mL/⅛fl oz raspberry syrup
top up with soda

Method

Shake over ice and strain then top up with
soda. Garnish with assorted colorful
cherries.

Czech Republic

Candy Cane

Ingredients
Glass: 285mL/9½oz Tall Wine Glass
Mixers: dash Grenadine
           30mL/1fl oz white Crème de Cacao
           30mL/1fl oz peppermint liqueur
           30mL/1fl oz sweet 'n' sour
           2 scoops vanilla ice cream

Method
Blend all ingredients with ice and strain.
Sprinkle with peppermint chocolate.
Comment: sweet 'n' sour is made from an equal mix of lemon juice and lime juice.

Cape Kennedy

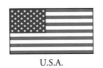

U.S.A.

Ingredients
Glass: 90mL/3oz Cocktail glass
Mixers: 5mL/⅛fl oz dark rum
           30mL/1fl oz lemon juice
           5mL/⅛fl oz Scotch whiskey
           30mL/1fl oz orange juice
           5mL/⅛fl oz Benedictine
           2-3 ice cubes
           5mL/⅛fl oz sugar syrup

Method
Shake and strain into 3 oz cocktail glass and serve.

Caper's Caper

U.S.A.

Ingredients
Glass: 300mL/10oz Colada Glass
Mixers: 30mL/1fl oz Advocaat
           ¼ Avocado
           30mL/1fl oz Frangelico
           1 scoop ice cream
           4-5 strawberries

Method
Blend ingredients with ice and pour into colada glass. Float coffee bean and serve with straws.

Careless Whisper

Switzerland

Ingredients

Glass: 90mL/3oz Cocktail Glass
Mixers: 30mL/1fl oz strawberry
liqueur
10mL/⅜fl oz cream
10mL/⅜fl oz Cheri-Suisse
20mL/⅝fl oz Amanda

Method
Shake and strain into cocktail glass,
garnish with grated chocolate, cherry
and serve.

Carlton

Canada

Ingredients

Glass: 90mL/3oz Cocktail Glass
Mixers: 30mL/1fl oz Canadian
whiskey
10mL/⅜fl oz orange juice
15mL/½fl oz Cointreau
cracked ice

Method
Shake and strain into cocktail glass
and serve.

Caribbean Champagne

Barbados

Ingredients
Glass: 140mL/5oz Champagne
Saucer
Mixers: 100mL/3½fl oz Champagne
10mL/⅜fl oz Bacardi
10mL/⅜fl oz banana liqueur
5mL/⅛fl oz orange bitters

Method
Stir without ice and strain. Garnish with a
slice of banana.

France

Champagne Cocktail

Ingredients
Glass: 140mL/5oz Champagne Flute
Mixers: 1 sugar cube
6 drops of Angostura Bitter
15mL/½fl oz cognac or brandy
top up with Champagne

Method
Soak sugar cube in Angostura Bitter in flute, before adding brandy, then top with Champagne. Garnish with a red cherry (optional).

Cha Cha

Italy

Ingredients

Glass: 90mL/3oz Cocktail Glass
Mixers: 30mL/1fl oz Frangelico
15mL/½fl oz cream
30mL/1fl oz Crème de Cacao

Method
Float ingredients in cocktail glass and serve.

Champagne Cocktail No.

United Kingdom

Ingredients

Glass: 140mL Champagne Saucer
Mixers: 15mL/½fl oz brandy
1 sugar cube
chilled Champagne
1 dash Angostura Bitter
1 dash orange curaçao

Method
Place sugar cube in a champagne saucer, add Angostura Bitter and curaçao. Fill almost to top with champagne, float brandy on top. Garnish with orange peel and serve.

Daiquiri - Kings

United Kingdom

Ingredients

Glass: 140mL/5oz Champagne
Saucer
Mixers: 45mL/1½fl oz white rum
15mL/½fl oz lemon juice
15mL/½fl oz Parfait Amour
¼ teaspoon sugar
1 dash egg white

Method
Blend with ice until smooth, pour into a champagne saucer and serve.

Daiquiri - Kiwifruit

New Zealand

Ingredients

Glass: 140mL/5oz Champagne
Saucer
Mixers: 30mL/1fl oz Bacardi light
rum
30mL/1fl oz lemon juice
30mL/1fl oz Cointreau
15mL/½fl oz sugar syrup
30mL/1fl oz Midori
½ kiwifruit

Method
Blend ingredients until smooth, pour into a champagne saucer and serve.

Daiquiri - Mango

Cuba

Ingredients

Glass: 210mL/7oz Fancy Cocktail
Glass
Mixers: 45mL/1½fl oz Bacardi rum
20mL/⅝fl oz lemon juice
30mL/1fl oz Cointreau
15mL/½fl oz sugar syrup
30mL/1fl oz mango liqueur
½ mango

Method
Blend until smooth and pour into cocktail glass and serve.

Daiquiri - Strawberry

Cuba

Ingredients

Glass: 210mL/7oz Fancy Cocktail
Glass
Mixers: 45mL/1½fl oz Bacardi rum
20mL/⅝fl oz lemon juice
30mL/1fl oz Cointreau
15mL/½fl oz sugar syrup
30mL/1fl oz strawberry
liqueur
10 strawberries

Method
Blend until smooth and pour into cocktail glass and serve. Garnish with half a strawberry on side of glass.

France

Death in the Afternoon

Ingredients
Glass: 140mL/5oz Champagne Flute
Mixers: 15mL/½fl oz Pernod
           Champagne

Method
Build, no ice.
Ernest Hemingway's favorite cocktail.
A bubbly occasion deserves this fully
imported French aphrodisiac mixer.

Death by Chocolate

U.S.A.

Ingredients

Glass: 210mL/7oz Old Fashioned
Mixers: 30mL/1fl oz Baileys Irish
           Cream
           30mL/1fl oz Crème de
           Cacao
           30mL/1fl oz Kahlúa
           90mL/3fl oz thickened
           cream
           30mL/1fl oz Tia Maria

Method
Shake and strain into a champagne
saucer, garnish with grated chocolate
and serve.

Deep Throat

U.S.A.

Ingredients

Glass: Whiskey Shot
Mixers: 20mL/⅝fl oz Kahlúa
           20mL/⅝fl oz Grand Marnier
           10mL/⅜fl oz cream

Method
Layer in order in a shot glass and
serve.

112

France

Depth Charge

Ingredients
Glass: 375mL/12½oz Beer Glass
Mixers: 330mL/11fl oz beer
            30mL/1fl oz Cointreau

Method
Pour beer into glass, fill a 1 oz shot glass with Cointreau. Drop shot glass into beer.

De Rigueur

Australia

Ingredients
Glass: 175mL/6oz Prism Rocks
Mixers: 30mL/1oz Scotch whiskey
            10mL/⅜fl oz grapefruit
            juice
            10mL/⅜fl oz honey

Method
Shake over ice and pour. Garnish with a swizzle stick.

Deshler

Canada

Ingredients
Glass: 90mL/3oz Cocktail Glass
Mixers: 30 mL/1 oz Canadian
            whiskey
            1 dash Angostura Bitter
            15mL/½ oz Dubonnet
            1 dash Cointreau

Method
Shake and strain into cocktail glass, garnish with lemon and orange peel and serve.

Devil's Handbrake

Thailand

Ingredients
Glass: Tall Dutch Cordial
Mixers: 15mL/½fl oz Banana Liqueur
15mL/½fl oz Mango Liqueur
15mL/½fl oz Cherry Brandy

Method
Layer in order.

Diplomat

Ivory Coast

Ingredients

Glass: 240mL/8oz Hi-Ball Glass
Mixers: 45mL/1½fl oz vodka
90mL/3fl oz pineapple juice
45mL/1½fl oz Midori
5mL/⅛fl oz lemon juice

Method
Shake and strain into a hi-ball glass
and serve with straws.

Dirty Mother

Mexico

Ingredients

Glass: 300mL/10oz Hi-Ball Glass
Mixers: 30mL/1fl oz tequila
milk
30mL/1fl oz Tia Maria

Method
Shake and strain over ice in a hi-ball
glass, top with milk and serve.

Mexico

El Diablo

Ingredients
Glass: 285mL/9½oz Hi-Ball Glass
Mixers: 30mL/1fl oz tequila
            15mL/½fl oz Crème de Cassis
            10mL/⅜fl oz lime juice
            top up with ginger ale

Method
Build over ice and top up with ginger ale.
Garnish with puréed lime.

Eldorado

U.S.A.

Ingredients
Glass: 120mL/4oz Cocktail Glass
Mixers: 30mL/1fl oz white rum
            30mL/1fl oz Advocaat
            30mL/1fl oz Crème de
            Cacao

Method
Shake and strain into cocktail glass
and serve. Garnish with grated
coconut.

Electric Blue

Iceland

Ingredients
Glass: 300mL/10oz Hi-Ball Glass
Mixers: 15mL/½fl oz vodka
            30mL/1fl oz dry vermouth
            15mL/½fl oz Blue Curaçao
            lemonade

Method
Pour vodka, vermouth and curaçao
over ice in hi-ball glass. Top with
lemonade and serve.

Esme's Peril

Cuba

Ingredients

Glass: Tankard
Mixers: 90mL/3fl oz Bacardi rum
60mL/2fl oz lemon juice
30mL/1fl oz dark rum
30mL/1fl oz orange juice
2 tablespoons banana liqueur
3 tablespoons cream
½ banana
2 teaspoon sugar
4 strawberries

Method
Blend all ingredients until smooth, pour into a tankard and serve.

Eton Blazer

United Kingdom

Ingredients

Glass: 300mL/10oz Hi-Ball Glass
Mixers: 30mL/1fl oz gin
15mL/½fl oz lemon juice
30mL/1fl oz kirsch
soda water
2 teaspoons sugar syrup
2 Maraschino cherries

Method
Place ingredients except soda and Cherries in hi-ball glass, top with soda, garnish with Maraschino cherries and serve.

Evergreen

Ireland

Ingredients
Glass: 90mL/3oz Cocktail Glas
Mixers: 15mL/½fl oz dry vermouth
30mL/1fl oz gin
15mL/½fl oz Midori
10mL/⅜fl oz Blue Curaçao

Method
Stir over ice and strain.
Garnish with red cherry on lip of glass.
Stir the first three ingredients of this pre dinner cocktail over ice and strain into cocktail glass. Then drop the Blue Curaçao creating a visible layer. A poignant tasting cocktail consumed in summer.

Flying Carpet

Saudi Arabia

Ingredients

Glass: 90mL/3oz Cocktail Glass
Mixers: 30mL/1fl oz vodka
15mL/½fl oz banana liqueur
15mL/½fl oz Advocaat
30mL/1fl oz cream

Method
Shake and strain into cocktail glass and serve.

Flying High

France

Ingredients

Glass: 90mL/3oz Cocktail Glass
Mixers: 30mL/1fl oz Baileys Irish Cream
15mL/½fl oz Drambuie
30mL/1fl oz Cointreau

Method
Shake and strain into cocktail glass and serve.

Netherlands

Flying Dutchman

Ingredients
Glass: 180mL/6oz Old Fashioned Spirit Glass
Mixers: 10mL/⅜fl oz Cointreau
30mL/1fl oz Gilbey's Gin

Method
Coat glass with Cointreau then pour Gilbey's Gin over ice. Garnish with a lemon twist.

Austria

Fog Cutter

Ingredients
Glass: 285mL/9½fl oz Hi-Ball Glass
Mixers: 15mL/½fl oz dark rum
              10mL/⅜fl oz brandy
              15mL/½fl oz Orgeat
              30mL/1fl oz lemon juice
              150mL/5fl oz orange juice

Method
Shake over ice and pour. Garnish with a strawberry.
Orgeat is an almond-flavored non-alcoholic syrup. Amaretto may be used as a substitute.

Forty Winks

New Zealand

Ingredients

Glass: Whiskey Prism Shot Glass
Mixers: 1 teaspoon honey
              15mL/½fl oz peach liqueur
              15mL/½fl oz orange curaçao
              4-5 drops Grenadine

Method
Pour peach liqueur onto honey, layer orange curaçao, then drop Grenadine.

Forth of July

U.S.A.

Ingredients

Glass: 285mL/9½fl oz Hi-Ball Glass
Mixers: 30mL/1fl oz bourbon
              orange juice
              30mL/1fl oz Kahlúa
              cream
              Galleon Liverno

Method
Place bourbon and Kahlúa in hi-ball glass. Fill to 2.5cm/1 inch from top with orange juice and add cream. Float Galleon Liverno on top and serve.

401

Luxembourg

Ingredients

Glass: Cordial (Lexington)
Mixers: 10mL/⅜fl oz Kahlúa
5mL/⅛fl oz Baileys Irish Cream
10mL/⅜fl oz banana liqeur
5mL/⅛fl oz Cointreau

Method

Layer in order in shot glass and serve.

Fraise Année

France

Ingredients

Glass: 120mL/4oz Cocktail Glass
Mixers: 30mL/1fl oz strawberry liqueur
45mL/1½fl oz cream
30mL/1fl oz white Crèam de Cacao
15mL/½fl oz brandy

Method

Blend ingredients and pour into a colada glass. Garnish with a strawberry and serve.

Franjelico Luau

Italy

Ingredients

Glass: 285mL/9½fl oz Hi-Ball Glass
Mixers: 45mL/1½fl oz Frangelico
210mL/7fl oz pineapple juice
dash of Grenadine

Method

Blend with ice and pour. Garnish with a pineapple slice and leaves.

Frappe

U.S.A.

Ingredients

Glass: 90mL/3oz Cocktail Glass
Mixers: quantity of preferred liqueur
(e.g. green Crème de
Menthe liqueur)

Method
Build over crushed ice. Two short
straws.
Spoon the required quantity of crushed
ice into the glass. Create spectacular
rainbow effects with small quantities of
liqueurs. Green Crème de Menthe is
highly recommended because it acts
as a breath freshener after dessert.

Frappe Byrrh

U.S.A.

Ingredients

Glass: 90mL/3oz Cocktail Glass
Mixers: 60mL/1fl oz Byrrh

Method
Fill cocktail glass with crushed ice and
pour Byrrh over ice. Garnish with
lemon twist and serve.

Galliano Hot Shot

Italy

Ingredients

Glass: Whiskey Shot
Mixers: 15mL/½fl oz Galleon
Liverno
5mL/⅛fl oz cream (float)
25mL/⅞fl oz hot black
coffee

Method
Top Galliano with black coffee in shot glass. Float cream and serve.

Garden City

India

Ingredients

Glass: 150mL/5oz Cocktail Glass
Mixers: 60mL/2fl oz brandy
30mL/1fl oz orange juice
30mL/1fl oz sweet
vermouth
15mL/½fl oz Pernod

Method
Shake and strain into cocktail glass, garnish with Maraschino cherry and serve.

Japan

Geisha

Ingredients
Glass: 135mL/4½oz Tulip Champagne
Glass
Mixers: 30mL/1fl oz Bourbon
30mL/1fl oz sake
10mL/⅜fl oz lemon juice
10mL/⅜fl oz sugar syrup

Method
Shake over ice and strain. Garnish with a red cherry.

Geisha Delight

Japan

Ingredients

Glass: 140mL/5oz Tulip
          Champagne Glass
Mixers: 30mL/1fl oz Midori
          5mL/⅛fl oz coconut rum
          15mL/½fl oz Galliano
          60mL/2fl oz pineapple juice
          15mL/½fl oz Cointreau

Method
Shake over ice and strain. Garnish with
a red cherry.

Genoa

Italy

Ingredients

Glass: 200mL/7oz Gilbraltar
          Hi-Ball Glass
Mixers: 30mL/1fl oz sugar syrup
          30mL/1fl oz Bacardi
          30mL/1fl oz lemon
          juice

Method
Shake over ice and strain then add ice.
Garnish with olives.

Georgia Peach

U.S.A.

Ingredients
Glass: 285mL/9½oz Hi-Ball Glass
Mixers: 30mL/1fl oz Bacardi
          30mL/1fl oz peach liqueur
          90mL/3fl oz cranberry juice

Method
Build over ice and pour. Garnish with a
peach slice.

Germany

German Chocolate Cake

Ingredients
Glass: 285mL/9½oz Hurricane Glass
Mixers: 30mL/1fl oz Kahlúa
           30mL/1fl oz Malibu
           30mL/1fl oz chocolate syrup
           2 chopped pecan nuts
           2 scoops vanilla ice cream

Method
Blend without ice and pour over crushed ice. Garnish with shredded pecans.
More like a meal than a cocktail! From a country where eating and drinking are national pastimes, the Germans have created this delicious multi gastronomic after dinner delight.

Get Going

United Kingdom

Ingredients
Glass: 285mL/9½fl oz Hi-Ball
           Glass
Mixers: 45mL/1½fl oz gin
           30mL/1fl oz lemon juice
           1 dash sugar syrup
           1 dash Grenadine
           lemonade

Method
Half fill hi-ball glass with cracked ice. Add ingredients, top with lemonade, add straws and serve.

Ghetto Blaster

U.S.A.

Ingredients
Glass: Tall Dutch Cordial
Mixers: 10mL/⅜fl oz Kahlúa
           10mL/⅜fl oz rye whiskey
           25mL/⅞fl oz tequila

Method
Layer in a shot glass and serve.

Gibson

United Kingdom

Ingredients
Glass: 120mL/4oz Cocktail Glass
Mixers: 60mL/2fl oz gin
10mL/⅜fl oz dry vermouth

Method
Shake over ice and strain. Garnish with one cocktail onion.

Gigolo's Delight

United Kingdom

Ingredients
Glass: 210mL/7oz Old Fashioned
Mixers: 30mL/1fl oz gin
60mL/2fl oz sweet vermouth
30mL/1fl oz orange juice

Method
Shake and strain over ice in a rocks glass. Garnish with 2 strips orange peel, Maraschino cherry and serve.

Gilroy

Switzerland

Ingredients
Glass: 90mL/3oz Cocktail Glass
Mixers: 15mL/½fl oz cherry brandy
10mL/⅜fl oz lemon juice
15mL/½fl oz gin
1 dash orange bitters
10mL/⅜fl oz sweet vermouth

Method
Shake and strain into cocktail glass and serve.

United Kingdom

Gimlet

Ingredients
Glass: 175mL/6oz Prism Rocks Glass
Mixers: 60mL/2fl oz gin
             30mL/1fl oz lime juice

Method
Shake over ice and pour then add cubed ice. Garnish with two cocktail onions on toothpicks sunk in glass.

Gin and It

United Kingdom

Ingredients

Glass: 90mL/3oz Cocktail Glass
Mixers: 30mL/1fl oz sweet
             vermouth
             45mL/1½fl oz gin

Method
Shake and strain into cocktail glass and serve.

Gin and Sin

U.S.A.

Ingredients

Glass: 210mL/7oz Old Fashioned
             Glass
Mixers: 60mL/2fl oz gin
             soda water
             30mL/1fl oz lime juice

Method
Shake ingredients except soda water and strain into an old fashioned glass. Top with soda water and serve.

Gin Twist

France

Ingredients

Glass: 140mL/5oz Cocktail Glass
Mixers: 30mL/1fl oz gin
1 dash orange bitters
30mL/1fl oz Dubonnet
10mL/⅜fl oz Pernod

Method
Shake and strain into cocktail glass.
Garnish with slice of orange and serve.

Ginger Sin

Lebanon

Ingredients

Glass: 300mL/10oz Hi-Ball Glass
Mixers: 30mL/1fl oz gin
30mL/1fl oz lime juice
ginger beer

Method
Stir ingredients and strain into a
hi-ball glass. Top with ginger beer and
serve.

Australia

Ginger Mick

Ingredients
Glass: 285mL/9½oz Footed Hi-Ball
Glass
Mixers: 120mL/4fl oz dry ginger ale
15mL/½fl oz lime juice
30mL/1fl oz Claytons Tonic
30mL/1fl oz lemon juice
60mL/2fl oz apple juice

Method
Blend with ice and pour.
Garnish with two banana wheel slices
wedged on rim of glass.

Girl Talk

U.S.A.

Ingredients

Glass: 140mL/5oz Cocktail Glass
Mixers: 45mL/1½fl oz white rum
1 dash Angostura bitter
15mL/½fl oz sweet
vermouth
15mL/½fl oz orange juice
15mL/½fl oz dry vermouth

Method
Half fill mixing glass with cracked ice.
Add ingredients and stir. Strain into a
cocktail glass. Garnish with cherry and
serve.

Globe Gladness

Austria

Ingredients

Glass: 300mL/10oz Hi-Ball
Glass
Mixers: 30mL/1fl oz Grand Marnier
1 dash Galleon Liverno
15mL/½fl oz schnapps
lemonade
15mL/½fl oz Tia Maria

Method
Shake Grand Marnier, Tia Maria and
schnapps. Strain into a hi-ball glass.
Top with lemonade. Float Galleon
Liverno and serve.

Glasgow

Scotland

Ingredients
Glass: 150mL/5oz Old Fashioned
Spirit Glass
Mixers: 30mL/1fl oz Scotch whisky
10mL lemon juice
5mL/⅙fl oz dry vermouth
5mL/⅙fl oz almond extract

Method
Shake over ice and pour then add cubed
ice. Garnish with shredded almonds and a
dried flower.

Italy

Godfather

Ingredients

Glass: 185mL/6oz Old Fashioned
Spirit Glass

Mixers: 30mL/1fl oz Scotch whisky
30mL/1fl oz Amaretto

Method
Build over ice. To be drunk as either a pre dinner drink or a night-cap. The guiding hand of Amaretto tempers the boldness of the Scotch.

Goddaughter

Ingredients

Italy

Glass: 140mL/5oz Champagne
Saucer

Mixers: 30mL/1fl oz Sambucca
30mL/1fl oz cream
30mL/1fl oz Amaretto
5mL/⅛fl oz Grenadine

Method
Shake ingredients and strain into a champagne saucer. Garnish with chocolate, strawberry and a sprig of mint.

Godmother

Ingredients

Italy

Glass: 185mL/6oz Old Fashioned
Glass

Mixers: 45mL/1½fl oz vodka
20mL/⅝fl oz Amaretto

Method
Build into a old fashioned glass filled with ice and serve.

Gold Passion

Spain

Ingredients

Glass: 185mL/6oz Old Fashioned
Mixers: 30mL/1fl oz Bacardi rum
chilled pineapple juice
30mL/1fl oz vodka
30mL/1fl oz passionfruit

Method
Pour ingredients over ice in an old fashioned glass and top with pineapple juice. Garnish with a slice of pineapple, pineapple leaves, cherry and serve.

Golden

Cuba

Ingredients

Glass: 300mL/10oz Hi-Ball Glass
Mixers: 60mL/2fl oz Bacardi rum
1 egg yolk
1 teaspoon sugar
60mL/2fl oz lemon juice
soda water

Method
Shake ingredients except soda water and strain over ice in hi-ball glass. Top with soda water, add straws and serve.

U.S.A.

Golden Cadillac

Ingredients
Glass: 140mL/5oz Cocktail Glass
Mixers: 30mL/1fl oz Galliano
30mL/1fl oz white Crème de Cacao
30mL/1fl oz cream

Method
Shake with ice and strain.
Garnish with red cherry or strawberry.

Golden Dream

U.S.A.

Ingredients

Glass: 140mL/5oz Cocktail Glass
Mixers: 20mL/⅝fl oz Galliano
20mL/⅝fl oz Cointreau
20mL/⅝fl oz orange juice
20mL/⅝fl oz cream

Method

Shake with ice and strain.
Garnish with a red cherry on a toothpick on side of glass.
Chilled orange juice tarts the Galliano and freezes the Cointreau leaving a creamy, tangy lining from your throat to your toes. Cointreau may be replaced with triple sec.

Golden Dream No. 2

U.S.A.

Ingredients

Glass: 150mL/5fl oz Cocktail Glass
Mixers: 30mL/1fl oz brandy
15mL/½fl oz lemon juice
30mL/1fl oz Grand Marnier
60mL/2fl oz orange juice

Method

Shake and strain into cocktail glass and serve.

Golden Dragon

China

Ingredients

Glass: 90mL/3fl oz Cocktail Glass
Mixers: 30mL/1fl oz Galliano
20mL/⅝fl oz white curaçao
20mL/⅝fl oz cream
1 dash egg white

Method

Shake and strain into a cocktail glass and serve.

Golden Orchid

China

Ingredients

Glass: 150mL/5fl oz Cocktail Glass
Mixers: 30mL/1fl oz Scotch whiskey
15mL/½fl oz Maraschino
30mL/1fl oz Advocaat

Method

Shake and strain into cocktail glass and serve.

Golden Shot

Chile

Ingredients

Glass: 185mL/6oz Old Fashioned
Mixers: 30mL/1fl oz Scotch whiskey
90mL/3fl oz orange juice
1 egg yolk

Method

Blend and pour into a rocks glass and serve.

Golden Slipper

Turkey

Ingredients

Glass: 90mL/3oz Cocktail Glass
Mixers: 30mL/1fl oz yellow Chartreuse
10mL/⅜fl oz apricot brandy
1 egg yolk

Method

Shake over ice and strain.

Greek Buck

Greece

Ingredients

Glass: 285mL/9½oz Tall Wine Glass
Mixers: 30mL/1fl oz brandy
              10mL/⅜fl oz lemon juice
              top up with ginger ale
              10mL/⅜fl oz ouzo

Method
Shake brandy with lemon juice and top up with ginger ale then float ouzo. Garnish with a lemon slice.

Greece

Greek God

Ingredients
Glass: Whisky Shot
Mixers: 15mL/½fl oz ouzo
              15mL/½fl oz Pernod

Method
Pour in order then shoot.

Green Back

Ingredients
Glass: 90mL/3oz Cocktail Glass
Mixers: 30mL/1fl oz gin
10mL/⅜fl oz lime juice
10mL/⅜fl oz green Crème de Menthe

Method
Stir over ice and pour. Garnish with a lime slice (optional).

Green

Saudi Arabia

Ingredients
Glass: 300mL/10oz High-Ball Glass
Mixers: 15mL/½fl oz Crème de Menthe
30mL/1fl oz lemon juice
60mL/2fl oz gin
1 egg white
10mL/⅜fl oz sugar syrup
soda water

Method
Shake all ingredients except soda water and strain over ice in hi-ball glass. Top with soda water, add straws and serve.

Green Devil

Germany

Ingredients
Glass: 120mL/4oz Cocktail Glass
Mixers: 45mL/1½fl oz vodka
45mL/1½fl oz Crème de Menthe
30mL/1fl oz lemon juice

Method
Mix and strain into a cocktail glass, garnish with lemon peel and serve.

Green Eyes

Maldives

Ingredients

Glass: 300mL/10oz Hi-Ball Glass
Mixers: 30mL/1fl oz Midori
15mL/½fl oz coconut milk
30mL/1fl oz dark rum
15mL/½fl oz lime juice
45mL/1½fl oz pineapple
juice

Method

Blend ingredients and pour into a
hi-ball glass. Garnish with pineapple
wedge, straws and serve.

Green Paradise

Bermuda

Ingredients

Glass: 150mL/5oz Cocktail Glass
Mixers: 45mL/1½fl oz Midori
15mL/½fl oz orange juice
20mL/⅝fl oz Cointreau
15mL/½fl oz pineapple juice
10mL/⅜fl oz lemon juice
1 scoop crushed ice
Grenadine

Method

Blend all ingredients except Grenadine
until frozen. Place a dash of Grenadine
in the bottom of cocktail glass. Pour in
frozen ingredients and serve.

Green Slime

Greenland

Ingredients

Glass: Whiskey Shot
Mixers: 20mL/⅝fl oz melon liqueur
15mL/½fl oz vodka
5mL/⅛fl oz egg white

Method

Pour in order, then stir.
Add more egg white for greater slime.
Melon will keep the taste buds occupied,
vodka dilutes the egg white.

Green With Envy

Zimbabwe

Ingredients
Glass: 210mL/7oz Hurricane Glass
Mixers: 30mL/1fl oz ouzo
            30mL/1fl oz Blue Curaçao
            120mL/4fl oz pineapple juice

Method
Shake with ice and pour.
Garnish with pineapple spear with leaves and cherry. Serve with straws.
An afternoon cocktail. The aniseed in ouzo chills the pungent pineapple juice. As they say... "Jealousy's a curse, Envy is worse."

Green Slammer

Canada

Ingredients

Ingredients
Glass: 150mL/5oz Cocktail Glass
Mixers: 45mL/1½fl oz vodka
            30mL/1fl oz lemon juice
            30mL/1fl oz Midori
            15mL/½fl oz Galliano

Method
Shake and strain into cocktail glass, garnish with a lemon wheel and serve.

Greenhorn

South Africa

Ingredients

Glass: 300mL/10oz Hi-Ball Glass
Mixers: 60mL/1 oz Crème de
            Menthe
            soda water
            20mL/⅝fl oz lemon juice

Method
Shake all ingredients except soda water over ice into hi-ball glass. Top with soda water, add straws and serve.

Greenpeace Sorbet

New Zealand

Ingredients

Glass: 150mL/5oz Cocktail Glass
Mixers: 30mL/1fl oz Cointreau
           1 kiwifruit (peeled)
           60mL/2fl oz white wine
           2 scoops crushed ice

Method
Blend until smooth and pour into a 5 oz cocktail glass and serve.

Gringo

Malta

Ingredients

Glass: 150mL/5oz Cocktail Glass
Mixers: 30mL/1fl oz tequila
           30mL/1fl oz vodka
           30mL/1fl oz Midori
           10mL/⅜fl oz lemon juice

Method
Shake and strain into cocktail glass and serve.

India

Gypsy King

Ingredients

Glass: Cordial (Lexington)
Mixers: 5mL/⅛fl oz lime cordial
           10mL/⅜fl oz Parfait Amour
           10mL/⅜fl oz green Crème de Menthe
           10mL/⅜fl oz yellow Chartreuse

Method
Pour in order, then layer yellow Chartreuse.

Hair of the Dog

Scotland

Ingredients

Glass: 185mL/6oz Old Fashioned
Mixers: 30mL/1fl oz Scotch
whiskey
30mL/1fl oz honey
60mL/2fl oz cream
ice

Method
Fill an old fashioned glass with ice,
shake other ingredients and strain over
ice and serve.

Hairless Duck

United Kingdom

Ingredients

Glass: 300mL/10oz Hi-Ball Glass
Mixers: 30mL/1fl oz Advocaat
15mL/½fl oz Bacardi rum
30mL/1fl oz vodka
orange juice

Method
Shake Advocaat, vodka and rum
together and strain over ice in a
hi-ball glass. Top with orange juice,
add straws and serve.

United Kingdom

Half Nelson

Ingredients
Glass: Whiskey Shot
Mixers: 15mL/½fl oz Crème de Menthe
10mL/⅜fl oz strawberry liqueur
20mL/⅝fl oz Grand Marnier

Method
Layer in order, shoot.

Halo

Switzerland

Ingredients

Glass: 150mL/5oz Tumbler
Mixers: 30mL/1fl oz Sambucca
           lemonade
           30mL/1fl oz gin

Method

Place Sambucca and gin in tumbler.
Slowly top with lemonade and serve.

Harbour Mist

Singapore

Ingredients

Glass: 150mL/5oz Cocktail Glass
Mixers: 30mL/1fl oz banana liqueur
           15mL/½fl oz Blue Curaçao
           20mL/⅝fl oz Grand Marnier
           30mL/1fl oz cream

Method

Shake and strain into cocktail glass
and serve.

Harbour Lights

U.S.A.

Ingredients

Glass: Cordial (Lexington)
Mixers: 10mL/⅜fl oz Kahlúa
           10mL/⅜fl oz Sambucca
           10mL/⅜fl oz green Chartreuse

Method

Layer in order.

Australia

Hard On

Ingredients

Glass: Cordial (Lexington)
Mixers: 20mL/⅝fl oz Crème de Cafe
           15mL/½fl oz banana liqueur
           10mL/⅜fl oz cream

Method
Layer in order, shoot.

Hard On (Bloody)

Australia

Ingredients

Glass: 90mL/3oz Cocktail Glass
Mixers: 30mL/1fl oz Kahlua
           30mL/1fl oz strawberry
           liqueur
           30mL/1fl oz Baileys Irish
           Cream

Method
Layer ingredients in cocktail glass then
serve.

Hard On (Black)

Australia

Ingredients

Glass: 90mL/3oz Cocktail Glass
Mixers: 30mL/1fl oz black
           Sambucca
           30mL/1fl oz banana liqueur
           30mL/1fl oz Baileys Irish
           Cream

Method
Layer ingredients in cocktail glass then
serve.

U.S.A.

Harvey Wallbanger

Ingredients
Glass: 285mL/9oz Hi-Ball Glass
Mixers: 40mL/1⅜fl oz vodka
                125mL/4fl oz Orange juice
                15mL/½fl oz Galliano, floated

Method
Build over ice. Garnish with orange slice and cherry.
The local Hawaiian bartenders will tell you a visiting Irishman called Harvey pin-balled down the corridor to hotel room after a night out. Hence, he was known a "Harvey Wallbanger."

Harlequin

France

Ingredients

Glass: 150mL/5oz Cocktail Glass
Mixers: 30mL/1fl oz cognac
                15mL/½fl oz Grand Marnier

Method
Frost the cocktail glass with harlequin frosting - coffee and sugar combined. Stir and strain liquid ingredients into glass and serve.

Havana Club

Cuba

Ingredients

Glass: 90mL/3oz Cocktail Glass
Mixers: 40mL/1⅜fl oz Bacardi rum
                20mL/⅝fl oz sweet vermouth

Method
Shake and strain into a 3 oz cocktail glass and serve. Garnish with a Maraschino cherry.

Hawaiian Punch

Ingredients

Glass: 285mL/9½oz Hi-Ball Glass
Mixers: 20mL/⅝fl oz Southern Comfort
20mL/⅝fl oz Amaretto
15mL/½fl oz vodka
40mL/1⅜fl oz pineapple juice
40mL/1⅜fl oz orange juice
20mL/⅝fl oz lime juice
20mL/⅝fl oz Grenadine

Method

Shake over ice and pour then add Grenadine. Garnish with orange slice and a red cherry.

Hazy Cuban

Cuba

Ingredients

Glass: 210mL/7oz Old Fashioned
Mixers: 30mL/1fl oz Bacardi rum
30mL/1fl oz coconut cream
30mL/1fl oz milk
60mL/2fl oz pineapple juice

Method

Blend and pour into an old fashioned glass and serve. Garnish with 1 slice pineapple

Head Stud

Zimbabwe

Ingredients

Glass: 150mL/5oz Cocktail Glass
Mixers: 30mL/1fl oz Galliano
30mL/1fl oz Afrikoko
60mL/2fl oz cream

Method

Layer in cocktail glass and serve.

Health Farm

Morocco

Ingredients
Glass: 270mL/9oz Hi-Ball Glass
Mixers: 90mL/3fl oz pineapple juice
          2 slices cantaloupe melon
          90mL/3fl oz orange juice
          2 teaspoons honey
          ½ ripe banana

Method
Blend with ice and pour.
Garnish with cantaloupe wedge and swizzle stick.
A great drink for the health conscious.

Heartbraker

Canada

Ingredients

Glass: 24mL/8oz Colada Glass
Mixers: 30mL/1fl oz strawberry
          liqueur
          60mL/2fl oz cream
          15mL/½fl oz Tia Maria
          4 strawberries
          15mL/½fl oz Cointreau

Method
Blend until smooth and pour into a colada glass and serve.

Helen's Hangover

Ireland

Ingredients

Glass: 140mL Champagne
          Saucer
Mixers: 30mL/1fl oz Advocaat
          pineapple juice
          30mL/1fl oz Galliano

Method
Pour Advocaat and Galliano over ice in hi-ball glass. Top with orange juice, add straws and serve.

Egypt

Hellraiser

Ingredients
Glass: Whisky Shot
Mixers: 15mL/½fl oz melon liqueur
           15mL/½fl oz strawberry liqueur
           15mL/½fl oz black Sambucca

Method
Layer in order, shoot.

Hemmingway

France

Ingredients
Glass: 150mL/5oz Champagne
           Saucer
Mixers: 40mL/1⅜fl oz Cointreau
           40mL/1⅜fl oz grapefruit
           juice
           40mL/1⅜fl oz Bacardi rum
           sparkling white wine

Method
Shake all ingredients except white
wine, strain into a champagne saucer.
Top with sparkling white wine and
serve.

Highland Flying

Scotland

Ingredients
Glass: 300mL/10oz Hi-Ball Glass
Mixers: 30mL/1fl oz Scotch
           whiskey
           30mL/1fl oz orange juice
           30mL/1fl oz Kahlúa
           30mL/1fl oz cream

Method
Blend until smooth, pour over
ice in hi-ball glass. Add straws and
serve.

Honey Bee

France

Ingredients

Glass: 150mL/5oz Cocktail Glass
Mixers: 30mL/1fl oz brandy
            15mL/½fl oz honey
            15mL/½fl oz Galliano
            60mL/2fl oz cream
            15mL/½fl oz Grenadine

Method

Shake and strain into cocktail glass
and serve.

Honeyed Nuts

Australia

Ingredients

Glass: Brandy Balloon
Mixers: 30mL/1fl oz Frangelico
            30mL/1fl oz honey
            15mL/½fl oz Kahlúa
            120mL/4fl oz cream
            15mL/½fl oz Advocaat

Method

Blend ingredients and pour into
a brandy balloon rimmed with crushed
hazelnuts and honey
and serve.

Honey Tea

Scotland

Ingredients

Glass: 250mL/8oz Irish Coffee Mug,
            preheated
Mixers: 1 orange spice tea bag
            30mL/1fl oz Drambuie
            top up with hot water

Method

Pour in order then top up with hot water.
Garnish with a lemon twist.

Jellyfish

Brazil

Ingredients
Glass:	Cordial (Lexington)
Mixers:	10mL/⅜fl oz Blue Curaçao
	10mL/⅜fl oz Sambucca
	10mL/⅜fl oz Baileys Irish Cream
	2 dashes of Grenadine

Method
Layer in order and pour Grenadine. Watch out for sting at the end of this slippery shooter.

Jeune Homme

France

Ingredients
Glass:	90mL/3oz Cocktail Glass
Mixers:	30mL/1fl oz dry vermouth
	15mL/½fl oz Benedictine
	15mL/½fl oz gin
	1 dash Angostura Bitter
	15mL/½fl oz Cointreau

Method
Shake ingredients and strain into cocktail glass and serve.

Jersey Cow

United Kingdom

Ingredients
Glass:	290mL/9oz Old Fashioned Glass
Mixers:	180mL/6fl oz cola
	scoop chocolate ice cream

Method
Stir over ice.
Garnish with a teaspoon of grated chocolate over top.
A choc-cola delight.

South Africa

Joburg

Ingredients
Glass: 150mL/5oz Old Fashioned
           Spirit Glass
Mixers: 30mL/1fl oz Bacardi
           15mL/½fl oz Dubonnet
           3 dashes of Orange Bitters

Method
Shake over ice and strain then add ice.
Garnish with a twist of orange peel.

Joggers

France

Ingredients
Glass: 300mL/10oz Hi-Ball Glass
Mixers: 30mL/1fl oz Benedictine
           1 spiral lemon peel
           45mL/1½fl oz Cognac
           soda water
           15mL/½fl oz lemon juice

Method
Half fill hi-ball glass with ice, drop in
lemon peel and add lemon juice. Top
with Cognac, Benedictine, soda water
and serve with straws.

John Collins

U.S.A.

Ingredients
Glass: 300mL/10oz Hi-Ball Glass
Mixers: 30mL/1fl oz gin
           1 teaspoon sugar
           1 lemon, squeezed
           1 dash Angostura Bitter
           soda water

Method
Place all ingredients except soda water
and lemon in hi-ball glass and stir until
sugar is dissolved. Add soda water,
garnish with lemon slice and straws
and serve.

Jungle Stern

Philippines

Ingredients

Glass: 300mL/10oz Hi-Ball Glass
Mixers: 30mL/1fl oz Midori
4 pineapple pieces
15mL/½fl oz banana liqueur
pulp ½ passionfruit
3 pureed strawberries
scoop crushed ice

Method
Pour pureed strawberries down the side of hi-ball glass. Blend other ingredients and carefully add to the glass. Garnish with a cherry and pineapple leaves and serve.

Jungle Juice

Trinidad

Ingredients

Glass: 210mL/7oz Hurricane
Glass
Mixers: 45mL/1½fl oz white rum
30mL/1fl oz pineapple juice
45mL/1½fl oz Drambuie
30mL/1fl oz cream
45mL/1½fl oz coconut
cream
½ banana

Method
Blend until smooth, place in a champagne glass and serve.

U.S.A.

Jupiter Martini

Ingredients
Glass: 140mL/5oz Cocktail Glass
Mixers: 30mL/1fl oz gin
10mL/⅜fl oz dry vermouth
10mL/⅜fl oz Parfait Amour
10mL/⅜fl oz orange juice

Method
Shake over ice and pour. Garnish with a floating small strawberry.

Kahlúa Jaffa

Jamaica

Ingredients

Glass: 140mL/5oz Champagne
Saucer
Mixers: 15mL/½fl oz Kahlúa
15mL/½fl oz orange juice
15mL/½fl oz Scotch
whiskey
30mL/1fl oz cream

Method
Shake and strain into a champagne
saucer, top with mixture of cream and
Grand Marnier and serve.

Kakuri

United Kingdom

Ingredients

Glass: 90mL/3oz Cocktail Glass
Mixers: 30mL/1fl oz Pimm's no. 1
cup
5mL/⅛fl oz lemon juice
15mL/½fl oz mango liqueur
15mL/½fl oz bianco
vermouth

Method
Shake and strain into cocktail glass
and serve.

U.S.A.

Kamikaze

Ingredients
Glass: 140mL/5oz Cocktail Glass
Mixers: 30mL/1fl oz vodka
30mL/1fl oz Cointreau
30mL/1fl oz fresh lemon juice
5mL/⅛fl oz lime cordial

Method
Shake with ice and strain.
Garnish with red cocktail onion on a
toothpick in the glass.
Maintain freshness for larger volumes by
adding stained egg white. Mix in a jug and
keep refrigerated. For the hyper-active.
Cointreau may be replaced with triple sec.

Ketango

Argentina

Ingredients

Glass: 90mL/3oz Cocktail Glass
Mixers: 45mL/1½fl oz vodka
30mL/1fl oz apricot brandy
30mL/1fl oz lime juice

Method
Shake and strain into cocktail glass, garnish with mint and serve.

Keep Going

Chile

Ingredients

Glass: 300mL/10oz Hi-Ball Glass
Mixers: 30mL/1fl oz white rum
15mL/½fl oz grapefruit juice
15mL/½fl oz anisette liqueur
lemonade
30mL/1fl oz cola tonic
½ slice lemon
15mL/½fl oz lime juice

Method
Half fill hi-ball glass with cracked ice, shake ingredients and strain into glass. Garnish with slice of lemon, straws and serve.

Kelly's Comfort

Ireland

Ingredients
Glass: 285mL/9½oz Hi-Ball Glass
Mixers: 30mL/1fl oz Southern Comfort
30mL/1fl oz Baileys Irish
Cream
30mL/1fl oz milk
4 strawberries
15mL/½fl oz sugar syrup

Method
Blend over ice and pour. Garnish with a strawberry.

K.G.B

Russia

Ingredients

Glass: 185mL/6oz Old Fashioned Spirit
Glass
Mixers: 30mL/1fl oz Kahlúa
30mL/1fl oz Grand Marnier
30mL/1fl oz Baileys Irish Cream

Method
Build over ice.
The first letter of each of the ingredients
give this cocktail its name. A late night party
drink.

Spain

Kick in the Balls

Ingredients
Glass: 140mL/5oz Champagne
Saucer
Mixers: 30mL/1fl oz dark rum
30mL/1fl oz orange juice
30mL/1fl oz melon liqueur
30mL/1fl oz cream
15mL/½fl oz coconut cream

Method
Shake with ice and strain.
Garnish with two melon balls previously
marinated in the rum.
Float melon balls. Using a toothpick, eat
both balls together and you'll be sure to
feel a "Kick in the Balls." Refridgerate
melon balls to preserve their freshness.

Kings Cross Nut

Australia

Ingredients

Glass: Coconut
Mixers: 60mL/2fl oz brandy
30mL/1fl oz Tia Maria
1 coconut

Method
Remove the top from the coconut and remove milk. Place half the milk, ice, brandy and Tia Maria in a shaker. Shake, pour into coconut, dust with nutmeg and serve with straws.

Kir Royale

France

Ingredients

Glass: 140mL/5oz Champagne
Flute
Mixers: 15mL/½fl oz Crème de
Cassis
sparkling white wine

Method
Place Crème de Cassis in a flute glass, top with sparkling wine and serve.

France

Kir

Ingredients
Glass: 190mL/6oz Wine Goblet
Mixers: 15mL/1/2fl oz Crème de
Cassis
top-up with dry white wine

Method
Build, no ice.
A superb pre-dinner drink. Use cold dry wines. Do not spoil the drink by using more than 15mL/½fl oz of Crème de Cassis.

Australia

Kiwi

Ingredients
Glass: 285mL Hi-Ball Glass
Mixers: 1 kiwifruit
30mL/1fl oz Bacardi
30mL/1fl oz Midori
15mL/½fl oz Cointreau
45mL/1½fl oz lemon juice
dash sugar syrup

Method
Blend with ice. Garnish with slice of kiwifruit on side of glass.

Kiss My Asteroid

U.S.A.

Ingredients
Glass: 390mL/13oz Hurricane Glass
Mixers: 30mL/1fl oz Midori
pineapple juice
30mL/1fl oz Blue Curaçao
15mL/½fl oz Cointreau

Method
Build Midori, Cointreau and pineapple juice in hurricane glass. Add Blue Curaçao to one large scoop crushed ice and float it on top of the pineapple juice, add straws and serve.

Klu Klux Klanger

U.S.A.

Ingredients
Glass: 150mL/5oz Cocktail Glass
Mixers: 30mL/1fl oz white rum
30mL/1fl oz vodka
30mL/1fl oz Southern Comfort
lemonade

Method
Pour ingredients over crushed ice in a cocktail glass and serve

Lady Brown

United Kingdom

Ingredients

Glass: 150mL/5oz Cocktail Glass
Mixers: 45mL/1½fl oz gin
         20mL/⅝fl oz orange juice
         20mL/⅝fl oz Grand Marnier
         15mL/½fl oz lemon juice

Method

Shake and strain into cocktail glass.
Garnish with orange segments and
serve.

Lady in Red

U.S.A.

Ingredients

Glass: 140mL/5oz Champagne
         Saucer
Mixers: 30mL/1fl oz vodka
         10mL/⅜fl oz lemon juice
         30mL/1fl oz Rubis
         1 dash egg white
         10mL/⅜fl oz Grenadine
         4 strawberries

Method

Blend and pour into a champagne
saucer and serve.

Lady M

Australia

Ingredients

Glass: 285mL/9oz Hurricane Glass
Mixers: 45mL/1½fl oz Frangelico
         45mL/1½fl oz melon liqueur
         2 scoops vanilla ice cream

Method

Garnish with strawberry on side of glass
sprinkled with grated chocolate. Blend for
more than 20 seconds to thoroughly mix
ingredients. Be adventurous and try
various flavored ice-creams.

Lady Throat Killer

Philippines

Ingredients

Glass: Tall Dutch Cordial
Mixers: 10mL/⅜fl oz Crème de Café
          15mL/½fl oz melon liqueur
          10mL/⅜fl oz Frangelico

Method

Layer in order. This superb mixture offers an exquisite aftertaste.

Lady's Pleasure

United Kingdom

Ingredients

Glass: 140mL/5oz Champagne
          Saucer
Mixers: 60mL/2fl oz vodka
          1 dash egg white
          30mL/1fl oz Galliano

Method

Shake and strain into a champagne glass and serve.

Lambada

Brazil

Ingredients

Glass: Whiskey Shot
Mixers: 15mL/½fl oz mango liqueur
          15mL/½fl oz black Sambucca
          15mL/½fl oz tequila

Method

Layer in order.

Macauley

Canada

Ingredients

Glass: 300mL/10oz Hi-Ball Glass
Mixers: 30mL/1fl oz brandy
            1 orange wedge
            60mL/2fl oz curaçao
            30mL/1fl oz dry vermouth

Method
Shake and strain into hi-ball glass over ice and serve.

Macleay Street

U.S.A.

Ingredients

Glass: 140mL Champagne
            Saucer
Mixers: 30mL/1fl oz bourbon
            1 dash Grenadine
            15mL/½fl oz Galliano
            orange juice (top up)

Method
Shake and strain into a champagne glass, top with orange juice, stir and serve.

Japan

Madam Butterfly

Ingredients
Glass: 140mL/5oz Margarita Glass
Mixers: 1.   30mL/1fl oz Passoa
               15mL/½fl oz melon liqueur
               15mL/½fl oz white Crème
               de Cacao
               30mL/1fl oz pineapple
               juice
       2.   30mL/1fl oz cream
               15mL/½fl oz melon liqueur

Method
1. Shake with ice and strain.
2. Layer melon liqueur and cream.
Garnish: strawberry and butterfly.
Comments: This cocktail requires two shakers. In one hand, shake the first four ingredients over ice and strain. In the other hand, shake melon liqueur and cream, then layer.

Madras

India

Ingredients

Glass: 210mL/7oz Old Fashioned
Mixers: 30mL/1fl oz vodka
90mL/3fl oz cranberry juice
30mL/1fl oz orange juice

Method

Build over ice then top up float orange juice. Garnish with an orange slice.

Magnolia Blossom

U.S.A.

Ingredients

Glass: 90mL/3oz Cocktail Glass
Mixers: 30mL/1fl oz bourbon
20mL/⅝fl oz cream
20mL/⅝fl oz lemon juice
2 dashes Grenadine

Method

Shake then strain into cocktail glass and serve.

Mai-Tai

Tahiti

Ingredients

Glass: 285mL/9oz Hi-Ball Glass
Mixers: 30mL/1fl oz rum
30mL/1fl oz lemon juice
15mL/½fl oz Amaretto
30mL/1fl oz sugar syrup
½ fresh lime, juiced
30mL/1fl oz orange curaçao
Liqueur

Method

Shake with ice and pour.
Garnish with pineapple spear, mint leaves, tropical flowers if possible, lime shell.
Serve with straws.
A well known rum-based refreshing tropical cocktail. Grenadine is often added to redden a glowing effect while the rum may be floated on top when served without straws.

United Kingdom

Martini

Ingredients
Glass: 90mL/3oz Cocktail Glass
Mixers: 60mL/2fl oz gin
         10mL/⅜fl oz dry vermouth

Method
Stir over ice and strain.
Garnish with lemon twist or olive on toothpick in the glass.
The classically sophisticated black-tie cocktail. Always stirred; however, when shaken it is known as a "Bradford." An olive garnish retains the gin sting whereas a lemon twist makes the cocktail smoother.
Note: a "Dry Martini" has less vermouth.

Martin Luther King

U.S.A.

Ingredients
Glass: 300mL/10 oz Hi-Ball Glass
Mixers: 30mL/1fl oz vodka
         30mL/1fl oz gin
         cola

Method
Shake all ingredients except cola. Strain into hi-ball glass over ice. Top with cola and serve.

Mary Queen of Scots

Scotland

Ingredients
Glass: 140mL Champagne
         Saucer
Mixers: 30mL/1fl oz Scotch
         whiskey
         15mL/½fl oz Drambuie
         1 tablespoon castor sugar
         15mL/½fl oz green
         Chartreuse
         15mL/½fl oz lemon juice

Method
Dip the rim of a cocktail glass in lemon juice then in sugar. Shake Scotch whiskey, Drambuie and Chartreuse with ice and strain into rimmed glass. Garnish with cherry and serve.

Australia

Melon Avalanche

Ingredients
Glass: 285mL/9½oz Hurricane Glass
Mixers: 30mL/1fl oz Blue Curaçao
            30mL/1fl oz melon liqueur
            15mL/½fl oz triple sec
            60mL/2fl oz pineapple juice

Method
Pour Blue Curaçao into glass. Blend other ingredients with ice and pour.
Garnish with a triangle of pineapple on side of glass.

Melon Ball

New Zealand

Ingredients

Glass: 90mL/3oz Cocktail Glass
Mixers: 30mL/1fl oz Midori
            30mL/1fl oz strawberry
            liqueur
            30mL/1fl oz banana liqueur

Method
Float liquid ingredients in cocktail glass, place strawberry on lip of glass and serve.

Melon Rock

Australia

Ingredients

Glass: 210mL/7oz Colada Glass
Mixers: 60mL/2fl oz Midori
            60g/2oz honeydew melon
            30mL/1fl oz lemon juice
            10mL/⅜fl oz sugar syrup

Method
Blend and pour into a colada glass, garnish with 1 slice honeydew melon and straws and serve.

Melon Tree

Thailand

Ingredients

Glass: 300mL/10oz Hi-Ball Glass
Mixers: 30mL/1fl oz Midori
120mL/4fl oz milk
30mL/1fl oz peach tree
1 dash cream
30mL/1fl oz Galliano
1 scoop ice cream

Method
Blend and pour into a hi-ball glass
and serve with straws.

Merry Widow

Iceland

Ingredients

Glass: 140mL/5oz Cocktail Glass
Mixers: 60mL/2fl oz cherry brandy
60mL/2fl oz Maraschino
liqueur

Method
Shake and strain into cocktail glass,
garnish with cherry on lip of glass and
serve.

France

Ménage à Trois

Ingredients
Glass: 285mL/9½oz Hurricane Glass
Mixers: 30mL/1fl oz Pernod
30mL/1fl oz Malibu
60mL/2fl oz pineapple juice
15mL/½fl oz coconut cream
1 scoop orange sherbert
1 scoop vanilla ice cream

Method
Blend with ice. Garnish with a plastic
swizzle stick with three straws.
Voulez-vous soivez avec moi ce soir ?
When two's not enough company try this
genuine drink that originated from the
afternoon cocktail parties held on the
crowded houseboats lining the Seine
River in Paris. Ideal for three people.

Metropolis

Hong Kong

Ingredients

Glass: 180mL/6oz Old Fashioned
Mixers: 30mL/1fl oz Midori
            30mL/1fl oz Baileys Irish
            Cream

Method

Fill an old fashioned glass with cracked
ice, build ingredients and serve.

Mexican Berry

Mexico

Ingredients

Glass: 140mL Champagne
            Saucer
Mixers: 10mL/⅜fl oz Kahlúa
            10mL/⅜fl oz tequila
            10mL/⅜fl oz strawberry
            liqueur

Method

Layer in order in a shot glass
and serve.

Mexican Flag

Mexico

Ingredients

Glass: 140mL/5oz Champagne
            Saucer
Mixers: 60mL/2fl oz tequila
            10mL/⅜fl oz sugar syrup
            10mL/⅜fl oz lime juice

Method

Shake over ice and pour. Garnish with
green and white cocktail onions and a red
cherry across the glass on a toothpick.

Luxembourg

Mintlup

Ingredients
Glass: 310mL/10oz Hi-Ball Glass
Mixers: large sprig of crushed mint
           15mL/½fl oz lime juice
           90mL/3fl oz dry ginger ale
           90mL/3fl oz lemon & lime
           mineral water

Method
Build over ice.
Garnish with mint leaf on lemon slice.

Miss Aileen

Netherlands

Ingredients
Glass: 90mL/3oz Cocktail Glass
Mixers: 30mL/1fl oz Advocaat
           30mL/1fl oz Galliano
           30mL/1fl oz Vandermint

Method
Shake and strain into cocktail glass
and serve.

Mission Impossible

U.S.A.

Ingredients
Glass: 120mL/4oz Cocktail Glass
Mixers: 30mL/1fl oz Cointreau
           30mL/1fl oz Midori
           30mL/1fl oz strawberry
           liqueur
           30mL/1fl oz banana liqueur

Method
Layer in a 4 oz cocktail glass and
serve.

Mississippi Mud

U.S.A.

Ingredients

Glass: 140mL Champagne
Saucer
Mixers: 30mL/1fl oz Kahlúa
cola
30mL/1fl oz Southern
Comfort
1 small scoop ice cream

Method
Place Kahlúa, Southern Comfort and
ice cream in a 10 oz hi-ball glass. Top
with cola.
Sprinkle grated chocolate over the top.
Add two straws and serve.

Mocha Mint

Mexico

Ingredients

Glass: 90mL/3oz Cocktail Glass
Mixers: 20mL/⅝fl oz Kahlúa
20mL/⅝fl oz white Crème
de Menthe
20mL/⅝fl oz white Crème
de Cacao

Method
Shake with ice and strain. Garnish with
peppermint chocolate flakes.

Australia

Mockatini

Ingredients
Glass: 90mL/3oz Cocktail Glass
Mixers: 15mL/½fl oz lime juice
dash lemon juice
60mL tonic water

Method
Stir with ice and strain. Garnish with a
green olive on a toothpick or a lemon
twist.
The classic cocktail, non-alcoholic version.

Molfetta Madness

Belgium

Ingredients

Glass: 120mL/4oz Cocktail Glass
Mixers: 30mL/1fl oz Sambucca
           20mL/⅝fl oz cream
           30mL/1fl oz mandarin
           liqueur
           30mL/1fl oz orange juice

Method

Shake and strain into cocktail glass.
Garnish with orange slice and serve.

Monk's Madness

Thailand

Ingredients

Glass: 150mL/5oz Cocktail Glass
Mixers: 20mL/⅝fl oz cream
           strawberry liqueur
           60mL/2fl oz cream
           30mL/1fl oz Crème de
           Cacao
           cracked ice
           60mL/2fl oz Benedictine

Method

Shake and strain into cocktail glass
frosted with shaved chocolate.

Monkey Gland

Zimbabwe

Ingredients

Glass: 120mL/4oz Cocktail Glass
Mixers: 30mL/1fl oz gin
           10mL/⅜fl oz apple juice
           5mL/⅙fl oz Parfait Amour
           5mL/⅙fl oz Grenadine

Method

Shake with ice and strain
Garnish with an orange twist.
Variation: substitute 20mL Pernod for the
Parfait Amour and Grenadine.

Monkey's Punch

U.S.A.

Ingredients

Glass: Cordial (Lexington)
Mixers: 10mL/⅜fl oz Kahlúa
          15mL/½fl oz Crème de Menthe
          10mL/⅜fl oz Baileys Irish Cream

Method
Layer in order then shoot.

Monaco

Monte Carlo

Ingredients
Glass: 90mL/3oz Cocktail Glass
Mixers: 30mL/1fl oz rye whisky
          10mL/⅜fl oz Benedictine
          2 dashes of Angostura Bitter

Method
Shake with ice and strain.

France

Montmartre

Ingredients
Glass: 90mL/3oz Cocktail Glass
Mixers: 10mL/⅜fl oz Cointreau
30mL/1fl oz Gilbey's Gin
10mL/⅜fl oz Cinzano Sweet
Vermouth

Method
Coat glass with Cointreau then pour
gin Gilbey's Gin andsweet vermouth
Cinzano Sweet Vermouth over ice.
Garnish with a red cherry.
From the world renowned painters
courtyard next to Sacré Coeur that
overlooks Paris.

Moomba

Australia

Ingredients
Glass: 150mL/5oz Champagne
Saucer
Mixers: 30mL/1fl oz Bacardi rum
1 dash Grenadine
30mL/1fl oz Grand Marnier
15mL/½fl oz orange juice
10mL/⅜fl oz lemon juice

Method
Shake and strain into cocktail glass,
garnish with orange peel and serve.

Moonbeam

U.S.A.

Ingredients
Glass: 150mL/5oz Cocktail Glass
Mixers: 30mL/1fl oz Midori
30mL/1fl oz cream
20mL/⅝fl oz vodka
15mL/½fl oz Grand Marnier

Method
Shake and strain into cocktail glass,
garnish with kiwifruit and serve.

Moon Crater

Finland

Ingredients

Glass: 300mL/10oz Hi-Ball Glass
Mixers: 30mL/1fl oz vodka
           30mL/1fl oz Advocaat
           1 Maraschino cherry
           orange soda
           fresh cream (float)

Method

Place vodka and Advocaat in a
hi-ball glass, top with orange soda.
Float cream, dust with nutmeg and
garnish with cherry and serve.

Morning Glory

Saudi Arabia

Ingredients

Glass: 300mL/10oz Hi-Ball Glass
Mixers: 30mL/1fl oz Scotch whisky
           30mL/1fl oz brandy
           10mL/⅜fl oz Pernod
           10mL/⅜fl oz white curaçao
           dashes Angostura Bitter
           top up with soda

Method

Shake with ice and pour then
top up with soda. Garnish with an
orange twist.

Moroccan Cocktail

Morocco

Ingredients

Glass: 90mL/3oz Cocktail Glass
Mixers: 30mL/1fl oz gin
           30mL/1fl oz Cointreau
           5mL/⅛fl oz orange curaçao

Method

Shake with ice and strain. Garnish with a
lemon wheel.

Moscow Mule

Russia

Ingredients

Glass: 285mL/9oz Hi-Ball Glass
Mixers: 30mL/1fl oz vodka
15mL/½fl oz lime cordial
top-up with ginger beer

Method

Build over ice.
Garnish with slice of lemon and mint, straws and swizzle stick.
A long, cool, refreshing cocktail. It tastes a lot better if the juice of half a lime is squeezed into the cocktail in place of the lime cordial.

Moulin Rouge

France

Ingredients

Glass: 140mL/5oz Champagne Saucer
Mixers: 30mL/1fl oz gin
20mL/⅝fl oz apricot brandy
20mL/⅝fl oz lemon juice
1 teaspoon Grenadine
sparkling white wine

Method

Shake and strain into a champagne saucer, top with sparkling white wine.
Garnish with orange slice and serve.

Mount Cook Sunset

New Zealand

Ingredients

Glass: 140mL/5oz Champagne Saucer
Mixers: 45mL/1½fl oz vodka
15mL/½fl oz lemon juice
15mL/½fl oz Maraschino liqueur
15mL/½fl oz orange juice
1 dash Grenadine

Method

Shake and strain into a champagne saucer and serve.

Mount Temple

Israel

Ingredients
Glass: 90mL/3oz Cocktail Glass
Mixers: 30mL/1fl oz Kahlúa
30mL/1fl oz Tequila
30mL/1fl oz Coconut Liqueur

Method
Build over ice.
Garnish with a dollop of cream
in centre of glass.

Mount Fuji

Japan

Ingredients
Glass: 140mL/5oz Champagne
Saucer
Mixers: 30mL/1fl oz gin
15mL/½fl oz lemon juice
10mL/⅜fl oz heavy cream
1 egg white

Method
Blend with ice and strain.
Garnish with a round slice of
banana and mint leaves.

Myra

U.S.A.

Ingredients
Glass: 90mL/3oz Cocktail Glass
Mixers: 15mL/½fl oz vodka
30mL/1fl oz dry red wine
15mL/½fl oz sweet
vermouth

Method
Place ingredients in a mixing glass and
stir gently. Strain into cocktail glass
and serve.

Napolean

France

Ingredients

Glass: 90mL/3oz Cocktail Glass
Mixers: 45mL/1½fl oz gin
           1 dash white curaçao
           1 dash Fernet Branca

Method
Stir and strain into cocktail glass and serve.

New Yorker

U.S.A.

Ingredients

Glass: 90mL/3oz Cocktail Glass
Mixers: 15mL/½fl oz gin
           1 dash Cointreau
           45mL/1½fl oz French vermouth
           15mL/½fl oz sweet sherry

Method
Stir and strain into cocktail glass and serve.

France

Negroni

Ingredients

Glass: 90mL/3oz Cocktail Glass
Mixers: 20mL/⅝fl oz Campari
           20mL/⅝fl oz sweet vermouth
           10mL/⅜fl oz gin

Method
Shake with ice and strain. Garnish with a twist of lemon and orange peel.

Australia

Nick's Health Drink

Ingredients

Glass: 290mL/9oz Poco Grande Glass
Mixers: 60mL/2fl oz V8 juice
60mL/2fl oz orange juice
120mL/4fl oz natural yoghurt

Method
Shake with ice and strain.

Nickel Fever

U.S.A.

Ingredients

Glass: 150mL/5oz Cocktail Glass
Mixers: 20mL/⅝fl oz Southern Comfort
45mL/1½fl oz cream
20mL/⅝fl oz Galliano
45mL/1½fl oz orange juice
10mL/⅜fl oz Blue Curaçao

Method
Shake and strain into cocktail glass and serve.

Night of Passion

France

Ingredients

Glass: 290mL/9oz Poco Grande Glass
Mixers: 60mL/2fl oz gin
20mL/⅝fl oz lemon juice
30mL/1fl oz Cointreau
60mL/2fl oz passionfruit juice
60mL/2fl oz peach nectar

Method
Shake and strain into a rocks glass and serve.

Israel

Noah's Ark

Ingredients
Glass: Cordial (Lexington)
Mixers: 10mL/⅜fl oz Blue Curaçao
            10mL/⅜fl oz cream
            10mL/⅜fl oz lemonade

Method
Shake Blue Curaçao with cream, then layer lemonade. Optionally, place half a lychee nut in glass before pouring.

Norman Conquest

France

Ingredients
Glass: 90mL/3oz Cocktail Glass
Mixers: 60mL/2fl oz Calvados
            10mL/⅜fl oz Grenadine
            20mL/⅝fl oz lemon juice

Method
Shake and strain into cocktail glass and serve.

Nude Bomb

Canada

Ingredients
Glass: Cordial (Lexington)
Mixers: 10mL/⅜fl oz Kahlúa
            10mL/⅜fl oz banana liqueur
            10mL/⅜fl oz Amaretto

Method
Layer in order in a shot glass and serve.

Orange Nog

Scotland

Ingredients

Glass: 285mL Hi-Ball Glass
Mixers: 1 egg
120m/4fl oz milk
120m/4fl oz orange juice
10mL/⅜fl oz sugar syrup

Method

Blend over ice and pour. Garnish with a sprinkle of ground nutmeg and twisted orange peel.

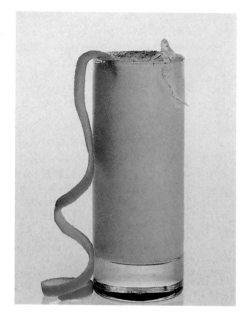

U.S.A.

Oramato

Ingredients

Glass: 240mL/8oz Footed Hi-Ball Glass
Mixers: 90mL/3oz tomato juice
120mL/4fl oz orange juice

Method

Shake with ice and pour. Garnish with an orange peel curl.

U.S.A.

Orgasm

Ingredients

Glass: 210mL/7oz Old Fashioned Spirit
           Glass
Mixers: 30mL/1fl oz Baileys Irish Cream
           30mL/1fl oz Cointreau

Method
Build over ice.
Garnish: Strawberry or cherries, optional
A "Multiple Orgasm" is made with the
addition of 30mL of fresh cream or milk.
A "Screaming Multiple Orgasm" has the
addition of 15mL Galliano along with 30mL
fresh cream or milk.

Orgasm Shooter

U.S.A.

Ingredients
Glass: Tall Dutch Cordial
Mixers: 20mL/⅝fl oz Baileys Irish
           Cream
           20mL/⅝fl oz Coinreau

Method
Layer in order then shoot.

Oyster Shooter

Australia

Ingredients
Glass: Cordial (Embassy)
Mixers: 10mL/⅜fl oz vodka
           10mL/⅜fl oz tomato juice
           5mL/⅛fl oz cocktail sauce
           Worcestershire Sauce to taste
           Tabasco Sauce to taste
           1 fresh oyster

Method
Pour tomato juice onto the vodka, float the cocktail sauce, dash sauces to taste and drop in oyster.
An early morning wake-up call, replenishing energy lost the night before. Also referred to as a heart starter.

Outer Space

Russia

Ingredients

Glass: 150mL/5oz Cocktail Glass
Mixers: 45mL/1½fl oz vodka
           10mL/⅜fl oz lime juice
           45mL/1½fl oz Bacardi rum
           20mL/⅝fl oz Galliano

Method
Shake and strain into cocktail glass, garnish and serve.

Pablo

Portugal

Ingredients

Glass: 90mL/3oz Cocktail Glass
Mixers: 30mL/1fl oz Bacardi rum
           10mL/⅜fl oz Cointreau
           1 Maraschino cherry
           10mL/⅜fl oz Advocaat

Method
Shake and strain into cocktail glass, garnish with pineapple, cherry and serve.

Paddy's Peril

Ireland

Ingredients
Glass: 150mL/5oz Cocktail Glass
Mixers: 60mL/2fl oz Baileys Irish
           Cream
           1 dash Grenadine
           30mL/1fl oz vodka
           crushed ice
           coconut milk

Method
Shake and strain into cocktail glass
and serve.

Paint Box

Netherlands

Ingredients
Glass: 90mL/3oz Cocktail Glass
Mixers: 30mL/1fl oz cherry
           Advocaat
           30mL/1fl oz Advocaat
           30mL/1fl oz Blue Curaçao

Method
Layer in cocktail glass and serve.

Cook Is

Pago Pago

Ingredients
Glass: 250mL/8oz Old Fashioned
Mixers: 30mL/1fl oz Bacardi Gold Rum
           10mL/⅜fl oz lime juice
           10mL/⅜fl oz pineapple juice
           5mL/⅛fl oz green Chartreuse
           5mL/⅛fl oz Cointreau

Method
Shake with ice and strain over 3 cubes of
ice. Garnish with a pineapple wedge and a
cherry.

Fiji

Palm Sundae

Ingredients
Glass: 285mL/9oz Hurricane Glass
Mixers: 45mL/11/2fl oz peach liqueur
           30mL/1fl oz coconut liqueur
           15mL/1/2fl oz banana liqueur
           60mL/2fl oz tropical fruit juice
           3 fresh strawberries

Method
Blend with ice and pour.
Garnish with orange wedge, pineapple leaves and Maraschino cherry.
Peach liqueur is dynamically exquisite in this specially designed cocktail recipe. The succulent peach flavor is another member in the new generation of natural tropical fruit cocktails.

Palm Tree

Mauritius

Ingredients
Glass: 150mL/5oz Margarita Glass
Mixers: 15mL/½fl oz Grand Marnier
           15mL/½fl oz mango liqueur
           15mL/½fl oz Cognac
           30mL/1fl oz cream
           15mL/½fl oz Bacardi rum
           15mL/½fl oz Malibu
           15mL/½fl oz peach liqueur

Method
Shake and strain into margarita glass, garnish with cherry, pineapple leaves and serve.

Palomino

U.S.A.

Ingredients
Glass: 150mL/5oz Cocktail Glass
Mixers: 20mL/⅝fl oz Galliano
           30mL/1fl oz Kahlúa
           45mL/1½fl oz cream

Method
Shake with ice and strain into cocktail glass and serve.

Plantation Night

Puerto Rico

Ingredients

Glass: 180mL/6oz Champagne Flute
Mixers: 30mL/1fl oz Kahlúa
30mL/1fl oz strawberry liqueur
30mL/1fl oz banana liqueur
1 banana
45mL/1½fl oz cream

Method
Blend until smooth and pour into a flute glass and serve.

Playground

U.S.A.

Ingredients

Glass: 90mL/3oz Cocktail Glass
Mixers: 30mL/1fl oz Baileys Irish Cream
30mL/1fl oz Malibu
30mL/1fl oz banana liqueur

Method
Layer in a cocktail glass and serve.

Nepal

Planters Punch

Ingredients
Glass: 150mL/5oz Cocktail Glass
Mixers: 30mL/1fl oz dark rum
30mL/1fl oz lemon or lime juice
60mL/2fl oz orange juice
5mL/⅙fl oz Grenadine

Method
Build over ice then add dash of Grenadine. Garnish with fruit slices.

Polish Sidecar

Poland

Ingredients

Glass: 90mL/3oz Cocktail Glass
Mixers: 20mL/⅝fl oz gin
            20mL/⅝fl oz lemon juice
            10mL/⅜fl oz blackberry liqueur

Method
Shake with gin and lemon juice with ice and pour then float blackberry liqueur. Garnish with blackberries or raspberries.

Tahiti

Polynesia

Ingredients
Glass: 135mL/4½oz Tulip Champagne Glass
Mixers: 30mL/1fl oz white rum
            30mL/1fl oz passionfruit liqueur
            10mL/⅜fl oz lime juice
            half egg white

Method
Blend with ice and pour. Garnish with passionfruit.

Port in a Storm

Portugal

Ingredients

Glass: 180mL/6oz Wine Goblet
Mixers: 45mL/1½fl oz port
⅜ strip orange peel
60mL/2fl oz red wine
15mL/½fl oz brandy
1 sprig mint

Method

Fill a large goblet glass with ice. Stir liquid ingredients and pour over ice. Garnish with sprig of mint and serve.

Porto Flip

Portugal

Ingredients

Glass: 150mL/5oz Cocktail Glass
Mixers: 45mL/1½fl oz port
1 egg yolk
10mL/⅛fl oz cognac
10mL/⅛fl oz sugar syrup

Method

Shake and strain into a cocktail glass, sprinkle with nutmeg and serve.

Prairie Oyster

U.S.A.

Ingredients

Glass: 90mL/3oz Cocktail Glass
Mixers: 30mL/1fl oz brandy
salt and pepper
Worcestershire Sauce
Tabasco Sauce
1 egg yolk

Method

Build, no ice.
The spices relieve a sore head and the brandy replenishes lost energy. Brandy may be replaced with any spirit of your choice, however cold vodka is medically soothing. Best before breakfast.

Pretty Woman

Australia

Ingredients

Glass: 285mL/9oz Hurricane Glass
Mixers: Blender 1
            30mL/1fl oz melon liqueur
            30mL/1fl oz Malibu
            Blender 2
            30mL/1fl oz strawberry liqueur
            3-4 strawberries

Method

Blend with ice in two separate blenders and pour. Garnish with strawberry and umbrella on side of glass.

Remember to tilt the glass when pouring the two sets of ingredients into the glass. Choosing a long glass will assist you. Very alcoholic as there is no juice.

A kaleidoscope of color for you to enjoy.

Wales

Prince of Wales

Ingredients

Glass: 150mL/5oz Champagne
            Saucer
Mixers: 15mL/½fl oz Madeira
            15mL/½fl oz brandy
            5mL/⅛fl oz Cointreau
            1-2 dashes of Angostura
            Bitter
            top up with Champagne

Method

Shake with ice and strain then top up with champagne. Garnish with an orange slice.

Purple Shell

United Kingdom

Ingredients

Glass: 150mL/5oz Champagne Saucer
Mixers: 60mL/3fl oz gin
15mL/½fl oz Parfait Amour
45mL/1½fl oz fresh cream

Method
Shake and strain into a champagne glass and serve.

Purple Waters

U.S.A.

Ingredients

Glass: 150mL/5oz Champagne Saucer
Mixers: 20mL/⅝fl oz Bacardi rum
15mL/½fl oz Parfait Amour
15mL/½fl oz orange curaçao
15mL/½fl oz yellow Chartreuse

Method
Layer in order in a cocktail glass and serve.

South Korea

P.S. I Love You

Ingredients
Glass: 150mL/5oz Champagne Saucer
Mixers: 30mL/1fl oz Amaretto
30mL/1fl oz Kahlúa
30mL/1fl oz Baileys Irish Cream
5mL/⅛fl oz Grenadine

Method
Build over ice and stir. Garnish with sprinkled nutmeg.

Puerto Rican Pink Lady

Puerto Rico

Ingredients

Glass: 135mL/4½oz Tulip Champagne
          Glass, sugar rimmed
Mixers: 30mL/1fl oz white rum
          10mL/⅜fl oz lemon juice
          10mL/⅜fl oz Grenadine
          half egg white

Method
Blend with ice and strain. Garnish with a
strawberry splashed with Grenadine.

Seychelles

Purple People Eater

Ingredients
Glass: 120mL/4oz Cocktail Glass
Mixers: 30mL/1fl oz Parfait Amour
          30mL/1fl oz gin
          10mL/⅜fl oz lemon juice

Method
Shake over ice and strain. Garnish with a
strawberry and pink parasol.

Canada

Quebec

Ingredients

Glass: 120mL/4oz Cocktail Glass

Mixers: 30mL/1fl oz Canadian Club Whisky
10mL/⅜fl oz dry vermouth
10mL/⅜fl oz Amer Picon
10mL/⅜fl oz Maraschino liqueur

Method
Shake over ice and strain. Garnish with a cocktail onion.
Amer Picon is a French brand of bitters that derives much of its flavor from gentian root and oranges. 3mL Angostura Bitter may be substituted.

Queen Bee

United Kingdom

Ingredients

Glass: 90mL/3oz Cocktail Glass
Mixers: 30mL/1fl oz gin
1 dash Pernod
30mL/1fl oz Cointreau

Method
Shake and strain into cocktail glass and serve.

Queen Elizabeth

United Kingdom

Ingredients

Glass: 90mL/3oz Cocktail Glass
Mixers: 30mL/1fl oz gin
15mL/½fl oz lemon juice
15mL/½fl oz Cointreau
1 dash Pernod

Method

Shake and strain into a cocktail glass, garnish with cherry and serve.

Queen's Peg

United Kingdom

Ingredients

Glass: 180mL/6oz Wine Goblet
Mixers: 30mL/1fl oz gin
1 large ice cube
sparkling white wine

Method

Place ice cube in a goblet glass, add gin and top with wine before serving.

Queen's

United Kingdom

Ingredients

Glass: 150mL/5oz Cocktail Glass
Mixers: 30mL/1fl oz gin
30mL/1fl oz pineapple juice
30mL/1fl oz dry vermouth
30mL/1fl oz sweet
vermouth

Method

Shake and strain into cocktail glass, garnish with cherry, pineapple wedge and serve.

Quenchie

Trinidad

Ingredients

Glass: 390mL/13oz Poco Grande
Glass
Mixers: 120mL/4fl oz orange juice
150mL/5fl oz lemonade
45mL/1½fl oz passionfruit pulp
45mL/1½fl oz white rum

Method

Build over ice and stir.
Garnish with a slice of orange, slice of lemon with 2 Maraschino cherries on toothpicks, serve with swizzle sticks and straws.

R & R

Australia

Ingredients

Glass: 90mL/3oz Cocktail Glass
Mixers: 30mL/1fl oz Cointreau
             30mL/1fl oz Midori
             30mL/1fl oz tequila

Method
Layer in order in a 3 oz cocktail glass
and serve.

Rabbit's Revenge

U.S.A.

Ingredients

Glass: 180mL/6oz Old Fashioned
Mixers: 45mL/1½fl oz bourbon
             tonic water
             3 dashes Grenadine
             30mL/1fl oz pineapple juice

Method
Shake ingredients except tonic water
and strain into an old fashioned glass.
Top with tonic water, garnish with
orange slice and serve with straws

Peru

Rabbit-Punch

Ingredients
Glass: Whiskey Shot
Mixers: 10mL/⅜fl oz Campari
             10mL/⅜fl oz dark Crème de
             Cacao
             10mL/⅜fl oz Malibu
             10mL/⅜fl oz Baileys Irish
             Cream

Method
Pour in order then layer Baileys.

Raffles Singapore Sling

Singapore

Ingredients

Glass: 285mL/9oz Hi-Ball Glass
Mixers: 30mL/1fl oz gin
30mL/1fl oz orange juice
30mL/1fl oz cherry brandy
30mL/1fl oz lime juice
15mL/½fl oz triple sec
30mL/1fl oz pineapple juice
dash Angostura Bitter
15mL/½fl oz Benedictine

Method

Shake with ice and pour. Garnish with orange slice, mint, a cherry, swizzle stick and straws.
This recipe is the original Singapore version. With its fruit juices. it tastes totally different from some gin slings commonly served in bars.

Raging Bull

Zimbabwe

Ingredients

Glass: 180mL/6oz Old Fashioned
Mixers: 30mL/1fl oz Afrikoko
30mL/1fl oz Sabra
milk (top up)

Method

Pour over ice in an old fashioned glass, top with milk and serve.

Raider

U.S.A.

Ingredients

Glass: Whiskey Shot
Mixers: 15mL/½fl oz Baileys Irish Cream
15mL/½fl oz Cointreau
15mL/½fl oz Grand Marnier

Method

Layer in order in a shot glass and serve.

Rolls Royce

United Kingdom

Ingredients

Glass: 90mL/3oz Cocktail Glass
Mixers: 30mL/1fl oz dry gin
10mL/⅜fl oz Benedictine
15mL/½fl oz dry vermouth
15mL/½fl oz sweet
vermouth

Method
Stir and strain into a 3 oz cocktail glass
and serve.

Roman Driver

Italy

Ingredients

Glass: 150mL/5oz Champagne
Saucer
Mixers: 30mL/1fl oz Galleon
Liverno
1 dash Grenadine
15mL/½fl oz vodka
20mL/⅝fl oz cream
20mL/⅝fl oz almond syrup

Method
Shake and strain into a champagne
saucer and serve.

Russia

Russian Tea

Ingredients
Glass: 250mL/8oz Irish Coffee Glass
Mixers: 4 teaspoons of ground tea
120mL/4fl oz orange juice
15mL/½fl oz lemon juice
45mL/1½fl oz vodka
1 cinnamon stick
whole cloves
sugar to taste

Method
Boil the cinnamon stick and whole cloves
in water for 2 minutes, add tea and allow
to simmer for 2 more minutes. Strain into
glass before adding juices, vodka and
sugar. Garnish with an orange slice.

Rusty Bucket

Portugal

Ingredients

Glass: 150mL/5oz Cocktail Glass
Mixers: 30mL/1fl oz port wine
cola

Method
Build over ice in cocktail glass.

Rusty Nail

Scotland

Ingredients

Glass: 180mL/6oz Old Fashioned
Mixers: 30mL/1fl oz Scotch
whiskey
30mL/1fl oz Drambuie

Method
Fill an old fashioned glass with cracked ice. Add ingredients
and serve.

Scotland

Rusty Nail No. 2

Ingredients
Glass: 180mL/6oz Old Fashioned
Mixers: 30mL/1fl oz Scotch whiskey
30mL/1fl oz Drambuie
lemon peel

Method
Fill an old fashioned glass with cracked ice and lemon peel. Add ingredients and serve.

Japan

Rusty Spade

Ingredients

Glass: 140mL/5oz Margarita Glass
Mixers: 1 mango
30mL/1fl oz strawberry liqueur
1 passionfruit
dash of cream
ice

Method
Blend with ice with strawberry fan on side of glass.

Ryans's Rush

Australia

Ingredients
Glass: Cordial (Embassy)
Mixers: 10mL/⅜fl oz Kahlúa
10mL/⅜fl oz Baileys Irish Cream
10mL/⅜fl oz rum

Method
Layer in order.
An easy one. Don't be lulled by the pleasant taste, this one has a real kick.

Sail Away

New Zealand

Ingredients

Glass: 150mL/5oz Cocktail Glass
Mixers: 30mL/1fl oz Midori
          30mL/1fl oz lime juice
          15mL/½fl oz peach liqueur
          1 dash lemon juice
          30mL/1fl oz vodka

Method
Shake ingredients and strain into
cocktail glass. Garnish with a lime
wheel and serve.

Saint Petersburg

Russia

Ingredients

Glass: 150mL/5oz Cocktail Glass
Mixers: 30mL/1fl oz vodka
          30mL/1fl oz Blue Curaçao
          lemonade (top up)

Method
Shake vodka and curaçao and strain
into cocktail glass. Top with lemonade
and serve.

Saint Moritz

Switzerland

Ingredients
Glass: 150mL/5oz Old Fashioned
          Glass
Mixers: 30mL/1fl oz schnapps
          30mL/1fl oz cream

Method
Build with ice. Garnish with a layer of
heavy cream.
Traditionally this drink is made with
Chambord (a raspberry flavored liqueur
from France) instead of schnapps.

Saint Vincent

St Vincent

Ingredients

Glass: 150mL/5oz Champagne
         Saucer
Mixers: 30mL/1fl oz gin
         30mL/1fl oz cream
         30mL/1fl oz Galliano
         dash Grenadine

Method
Shake and strain into champagne
glass and serve.

Sake Special

Japan

Ingredients

Glass: 90mL/3oz Cocktail Glass
Mixers: 30mL/1fl oz sake
         2 dashes Angostura Bitter
         60mL/2fl oz gin

Method
Mix ingredients in a mixing glass,
strain into cocktail glass and serve.

Saketini

Japan

Ingredients

Glass: 90mL/3oz Cocktail Glass
Mixers: 30mL/1fl oz gin
         10mL/⅜fl oz sake

Method
Shake over ice and pour. Garnish with an
olive.

Panama

Salty Dog

Ingredients
Glass: 285mL/9oz Hi-Ball Glass -
              salt-rimmed
Mixers: 45mL/1½fl oz vodka
              top-up with grapefruit juice

Method
Build over ice.
Slowly re-emerging as the long, cool cocktail it was renowned for in its heyday. Unfortunately, a limited number of bars stock grapefruit juice, which restricts availability. But as the saying goes "Every dog has his day." Straws are unnecessary, drink the cocktail from the salt rim.

Salubrious Salutations

Austria

Ingredients
Glass: 90mL/3oz Cocktail Glass
Mixers: 15mL/½fl oz Galliano
            15mL/½fl oz Benedictine
            15mL/½fl oz Drambuie
            30mL/1fl oz cream
            15mL/½fl oz gin

Method
Shake and strain into cocktail glass and serve.

Sambucca Shaker

Italy

Ingredients
Glass: 210mL/7oz Old Fashioned
Mixers: 30mL/1fl oz Sambucca

Method
Pour Sambucca then light. Cup your hand entirely over the rim while it flames, creating suction. Shake the glass, place under your nose, take hand from glass to inhale the fumes, then shoot.

Spain

Sangria

Ingredients

Glass: 180mL/6oz Wine Glass
Mixers: 20mL/⅝fl oz Cointreau
            20mL/⅝fl oz brandy
            20mL/⅝fl oz Bacardi
            orange, lime, lemon and
            strawberry pieces
            sugar syrup
            spanish red wine

Method
Pour in order.
Thinly slice orange and lime and place in bowl. Pour in sugar syrup and allow to stand for several hours. Add red wine.

Satin Pillow

United Arab Emirates

Ingredients
Glass: 150mL/5oz Cocktail Glass
Mixers: 5mL/⅛fl oz strawberry liqueur
            10mL/⅜fl oz Cointreau
            15mL/½fl oz Frangelico
            15mL/½fl oz Tia Maria
            20mL/⅝fl oz pineapple juice
            20mL/⅝fl oz cream

Method
Blend with ice and pour.
Cut a strawberry in half and place on side of glass then swirl cream over strawberry halves.

Saturday Night

Canada

Ingredients

Glass:	180mL/6oz Colada Glass
Mixers:	15mL/½fl oz banana liqueur
	60mL/2fl oz lemon juice
	30mL/1fl oz gin
	15mL/½fl oz Blue Curaçao
	60mL/2fl oz cream

Method

Shake and strain into a colada glass, garnish with lime wheel, cherry and serve.

Sayonara

Japan

Ingredients

Glass:	150mL/5oz Cocktail Glass
Mixers:	30mL/1fl oz Midori
	75mL/2½fl oz cream
	30mL/1fl oz Advocaat

Method

Shake well, strain into cocktail glass and serve.

Sweden

Scandinavian Glogg

Ingredients

Glass:	180mL/6oz Wine Glass
Mixers:	30mL/1fl oz vodka
	60mL/2fl oz red wine
	3 blanched almonds
	3 raisins
	grated orange peel
	1 dried fig
	4 cardamon seeds
	1 cinnamon stick
	1 clove
	1 sugar cube per serve

Method

Simmer all ingredients in a saucepan for a few minutes except for sugar cubes, then pour.

Shady Lady

Japan

Ingredients

Glass: 300mL/10oz Hi-Ball Glass
Mixers: 30mL/1fl oz Midori
30mL/1fl oz tequila
1 slice lime
90mL/3fl oz grapefruit juice
1 Maraschino cherry

Method
Shake and pour over ice in a hi-ball glass, garnish with lemon, lime, cherry and serve.

Shandy

U.S.A.

Ingredients

Glass: 300mL/10oz Beer Glass
Mixers: 150mL/5oz beer
150mL/5oz lemonade

Method
Half fill beer glass with lemonade, top with beer and serve.

China

Shanghai Punch

Ingredients
Glass: 350mL/12oz Fancy Hi-Ball Glass
Mixers: 30mL/1fl oz cognac
30mL/1fl oz dark rum
45mL/1½fl oz orange juice
20mL/⅝fl oz Cointreau
20mL/⅝fl oz lemon juice
almond extract
fresh tea
grated orange and lemon peels
cinnamon sticks

Method
Boil tea and add ingredients then stir.

Sheep's Head

New Zealand

Ingredients

Glass: 150mL/5oz Old Fashioned
Mixers: 15mL/½fl oz sweet
vermouth
45mL/1½fl oz bourbon
1 piece lemon peel
15mL/½fl oz Benedictine

Method
Stir and strain into a small tumbler
glass, garnish with lemon peel, cherry
and serve.

Sherry

United Kingdom

Ingredients

Glass: 90mL/3oz Cocktail Glass
Mixers: 30mL/1fl oz gin
30mL/1fl oz lemon juice
30mL/1fl oz sweet sherry

Method
Shake and strain into cocktail glass
and serve.

U.S.A.

Shirley Temple

Ingredients
Glass: 310mL/10oz Hi-Ball Glass
Mixers: 15mL/½fl oz Grenadine
ginger ale or lemonade to
top-up

Method
Build over ice.
Slice of orange, serve with swizzle stick
and two straws.
For a tangy variation to this drink try a
Shirley Temple No.2. Use the following:
60mL/2 fl oz pineapple juice to a glass
half full of ice. Top with lemonade, float
15mL/½fl oz passionfruit pulp on top and
garnish with pineapple wedge and cherry.

Shocking Blue

PNG

Ingredients

Glass: 300mL/10oz Hi-Ball Glass
Mixers: 30mL/1fl oz Blue Curaçao
           30mL/1fl oz lemonade
           30mL/1fl oz Midori
           30mL/1fl oz banana liqueur

Method

Fill a hi-ball glass with ice and gently layer ingredients. Garnish with lime wheel and serve.

Shooting Star

U.S.A.

Ingredients

Glass: 180mL/6oz Colada Glass
Mixers: 30mL/1fl oz Midori
           30mL/1fl oz cream
           30mL/1fl oz peach liqueur
           30g/1oz rockmelon
           15mL/½fl oz orange curaçao

Method

Blend until smooth and pour into a colada glass.

Short Leg

Belgium

Ingredients

Glass: 285mL/9oz Hi-Ball Glass
Mixers: 30mL/1fl oz Cointreau
           30mL/1fl oz gin
           60mL/2fl oz orange juice
           15mL/½fl oz lemon juice

Method

Build over ice.

Sicilian Kiss

Italy

Ingredients

Glass: 150mL/5oz Old Fashioned
Mixers: 30mL/1fl oz Southern Comfort
           30mL/1fl oz Amaretto

Method
Build with ice.

U.S.A.

Sidecar

Ingredients
Glass: 90mL/3oz Cocktail Glass
Mixers: 30mL/1fl oz brandy
           20mL/⅝fl oz Cointreau
           30mL/1fl oz lemon juice

Method
Shake with ice and strain. Lemon twist optional.
A zappy pre-dinner cocktail. The lemon juice purifies the brandy and ferments the Cointreau. Too much lemon juice will leave an acidic after taste.

Simply Peaches

U.S.A.

Ingredients

Glass: 240mL/8oz Colada Glass
Mixers: 45mL/1½fl oz peach liqueur
2 peach halves
30mL/1fl oz Cointreau
2 scoops ice cream
75mL/2½fl oz peach nectar

Method
Blend until smooth and pour into a colada glass. Float a small scoop of ice cream, add straws and serve.

Sing Sing

Malaysia

Ingredients

Glass: 150mL/5oz Cocktail Glass
Mixers: 60mL/2fl oz Scotch
whiskey
30mL/1fl oz sweet
vermouth
30mL/1fl oz orange
curaçao

Method
Stir and strain into cocktail glass, garnish with twist of orange peel and serve.

Australia

Slippery Nipple

Ingredients
Glass: Cordial (Embassy)
Mixers: 30mL/1fl oz Sambucca
15mL/½fl oz Baileys Irish
Cream

Method
Layer in order.
One of the originals, very well received.
Cream floated on the Baileys becomes a "Pregnant Slippery Nipple". Grand Marnier included makes a "Slipadicthome".

Slow Comfortable Screw

U.S.A.

Ingredients

Glass: 300mL/10oz Hi-Ball
Mixers: 30mL/1fl oz vodka
            15mL/½fl oz sloe gin
            15mL/½fl oz Southern
            Comfort
            orange juice (top up)

Method
Build over ice in hi-ball glass, top with orange juice and serve with straws.

Slow Comfortable Screw No. 2

U.S.A.

Ingredients

Glass: 300mL/10oz Hi-Ball
Mixers: 30mL/1fl oz gin
            60mL/2fl oz Southern
            Comfort
            120mL/4fl oz orange juice

Method
Shake and strain into a hi-ball glass, garnish with orange wheel, cherry, straws and serve.

Slyde Your Thigh

Australia

Ingredients
Glass: 180mL/6oz Fancy Old
            Fashioned
Mixers: 30mL/1fl oz banana liqueur
            30mL/1fl oz Crème de Cacao
            30mL/1fl oz Midori
            60mL/2fl oz cream

Method
Shake with ice and pour into old fashioned glass and serve.

Smog City

Mexico

Ingredients

Glass: 300mL/10oz Hi-Ball Glass
Mixers: 30mL/1fl oz tequila
60mL/2fl oz cream
30mL/1fl oz Crème de Cacao
cola (top up)

Method

Half fill a hi-ball glass with cracked ice, add liquid ingredients and lop with cola. Add straws, swizzle stick and serve.

Smooth Boy

Fiji

Ingredients

Glass: 90mL/3oz Cocktail Glass
Mixers: 30mL/1fl oz Midori
30mL/1fl oz coconut cream
15mL/½fl oz Tia Maria
330mL/1fl oz cream
75mL/2½fl oz pineapple juice

Method

Shake and strain into two cocktail glasses. Garnish with orchids (if available) and serve.

Australia

Snake in the Grass

Ingredients

Glass: 120mL/4oz Cocktail Glass
Mixers: 60mL/2fl oz Baileys
30mL/1fl oz Crème de Menthe
cream (optional)

Method

Shake with ice and pour into cocktail glass.

Snake Bite Shooter

Portugal

Ingredients

Glass: Cordial (Embassy)
Mixers: 20mL/⅝fl oz Crème de Cafe
           10mL/⅞fl oz green Chartreuse

Method

Layer in order and shoot.

Snake Bite

United Kingdom

Ingredients

Glass: 120mL/4oz Cocktail Glass
Mixers: 60mL/2fl oz gin
           60mL/2fl oz Crème de
           Menthe

Method

Shake and strain into cocktail glass.

Snoopy's Gleam

U.S.A.

Ingredients

Glass: 90mL/3oz Cocktail Glass
Mixers: 30mL/1fl oz bourbon
           15mL/½fl oz orange
           curaçao
           10mL/⅜fl oz Grenadine
           15mL/½fl oz orange soda
           (float)

Method

Shake and strain into cocktail glass,
garnish with orange peel, cherry and
serve.

New Zealand

Splice

Ingredients
Glass: 210mL/7oz Hurricane Glass
Mixers: 30mL/1fl oz melon liqueur
15mL/½fl oz Galliano
15mL/½fl oz coconut liqueur
30mL/1fl oz pineapple juice
30mL/1fl oz cream

Method
Blend with ice and pour.
Garnish with pineapple wedge and leaves on side of glass.

Special Cream Chocolate

U.S.A.

Ingredients
Glass: 285mL/9oz Hi-Ball Glass
Mixers: 60g/2oz plain chocolate
½ teaspoon cinnamon
30mL/1fl oz brandy
150mL/5fl oz whipped cream (float)
300mL/10fl oz milk

Method
Heat chocolate, milk and cinnamon, add brandy and pour into hi-ball glasses. Float cream and serve with straws.

Springbok

South Africa

Ingredients
Glass: Cordial (Embassy)
Mixers: 20mL/⅜fl oz passionfruit syrup
10mL/⅜fl oz green Crème de Menthe
5mL/⅛fl oz ouzo

Method
Layer in order.

United Kingdom

Spritzer

Ingredients
Glass: 185mL/6oz Wine Goblet
Mixers: dry white wine, chilled
          soda water

Method
Build, no ice.
"Wet the whistle" with a responsible
alcoholic alternative. Ladies prefer the
soda dilution although you may be asked
for lemonade.

Sputnik

Russia

Ingredients
Glass: 150mL/5oz Cocktail Glass
Mixers: 75mL/2½fl oz vodka
          10mL/⅜fl oz lemon juice
          30mL/1fl oz Fernet Branca
          ½ teaspoon sugar

Method
Shake and strain over ice in cocktail
glass and serve.

Squashed Frog

Australia

Ingredients
Glass: 90mL/3oz Sherry Glass
Mixers: 30mL/1fl oz Midori
          30mL/1fl oz Baileys Irish
          Cream
          10mL/⅜fl oz Advocaat
          10mL/⅜fl oz cherry
          Advocaat

Method
Stir in Advocaat and cherry Advocaat.
Float Midori and serve.

U.S.A.

Stars & Stripes

Ingredients
Glass: 300mL/10oz Fancy Cocktail
Mixers: 10mL/⅜fl oz Blue Curaçao
             Blender 1
             30mL/1fl oz Southern Comfort
             30mL/1fl oz Frangelico
             Blender 2
             30mL/1fl oz strawberry liqueur
             3-4 strawberries

Method
Pour Blue Curaçao into glass. Blend other ingredients with ice in 2 separate blenders and pour.
Garnish: sprinkle grated chocolate flakes over top and add a strawberry and USA flag to side of glass.

Steroid Blast

Canada

Ingredients
Glass: 150mL/5oz Cocktail Glass
Mixers: 30mL/1fl oz rum
             30mL/1fl oz vodka
             15mL/½fl oz tequila
             30mL/1fl oz Benedictine
             1 dash soda water

Method
Shake and strain into cocktail glass, top with soda water and serve.

Stimulation

Czech Republic

Ingredients
Glass: 150mL/5oz Cocktail Glass
Mixers: 30mL/1fl oz Baileys Irish Cream
             30mL/1fl oz Cointreau
             30mL/1fl oz Malibu
             15mL/½fl oz cream

Method
Layer in order in cocktail glass and serve.

Stinger

Switzerland

Ingredients

Glass: 90mL/3oz Cocktail Glass
Mixers: 30mL/1fl oz brandy
           10mL/⅜fl oz white Crème de
           Menthe

Method
Stir over ice and strain.

U.S.A.

Stormy Monday

Ingredients
Glass: 210mL/7oz Fancy Hi-Ball
Mixers: 30mL/1fl oz Southern Comfort
           30mL/1fl oz Malibu
           120mL/4fl oz orange juice

Method
Build over ice.

Surfers Paradise

Australia

Ingredients

Glass: 150mL/5oz Champagne Saucer
Mixers: 60mL/2fl oz vodka
15mL/½fl oz Blue Curaçao
45mL/1½fl oz dry vermouth
1 Maraschino cherry
20mL/fl oz Galliano

Method
Stir and strain into a champagne saucer, garnish with cherry and serve.

Surprise

United Kingdom

Ingredients

Glass: 210mL/7oz Old Fashioned
Mixers: 30mL/1fl oz gin
20mL/⅝fl oz apricot brandy
60mL/2fl oz orange juice

Method
Shake and strain over ice in an old fashioned glass and serve.

Sweden

Swedish Snowball

Ingredients
Glass: 210mL/7oz Old Fashioned
Mixers: 30mL/1fl oz Advocaat
15mL/½fl oz lemon juice
top up with soda water

Method
Build over ice then top up with soda. Garnish with a lemon slice.

Sweet Lady Jane

Thailand

Ingredients

Glass: 150mL/5oz Champagne Saucer
Mixers: 15mL/½fl oz Grand Marnier
            15mL/½fl oz orange juice
            15mL/½fl oz Cointreau
            15mL/½fl oz coconut cream
            30mL/1fl oz strawberry liqueur
            30mL/1fl oz fresh cream

Method
Shake with ice and strain.
Garnish with strawberry, mint and chocolate flakes.

Sweet Maria

U.S.A.

Ingredients
Glass: 150mL/5oz Old Fashioned
Mixers: 30mL/1fl oz bourbon
            30mL/1fl oz Tia Maria
            60mL/2fl oz cream

Method
Shake then strain into old fashioned glass.

United Kingdom

Sweet Martini

Ingredients
Glass: 90mL/3oz Cocktail Glass
Mixers: 45mL/1½fl oz gin
20mL/⅝fl oz rosso vermouth

Method
Stir over ice and strain.
Red cherry on toothpick in glass.
Sister to the "Dry Martini", the sweeter vermouth overwhelms the gin sting. A pre dinner cocktail which can be stirred and strained either:
"On The Rocks" - served in a standard Spirit glass over ice.
"Straight Up" - served in a 90mL/3 fl oz cocktail glass over ice.

Sweet Sixteen

New Zealand

Ingredients
Glass: 150mL/5oz Cocktail Glass
Mixers: 30mL/1fl oz gin
1 dash pineapple juice
15mL/½fl oz Malibu
1 dash coconut cream
15mL/½fl oz white Crème de Cacao
1 slice pineapple

Method
Blend until smooth and pour into a cocktail glass and serve.

Swiss Chocolate

Switzerland

Ingredients
Glass: 90oz/3oz Cocktail Glass
Mixers: 30mL/1fl oz anisette
fresh cream (float)
30mL/1fl oz cherry brandy
30mL/1fl oz green tea

Method
Pour ingredients into a cocktail glass, float cream, garnish with cherry and serve.

Talisman

Greece

Ingredients

Glass: 180mL/6oz Old Fashioned
Mixers: 30mL/1fl oz Midori
15mL/½fl oz lime juice
30mL/1fl oz orange juice

Method

Build ingredients in an old fashioned glass. Garnish with a lime slice in the glass and serve.

Temptation

Canada

Ingredients

Glass: 150mL/5oz Champagne Saucer
Mixers: 60mL/2fl oz rye whiskey
15mL/½fl oz Dubonnet
15mL/½fl oz Pernod
15mL/½fl oz white curaçao

Method

Stir and strain into a champagne saucer. Garnish with a twist of orange peel and serve.

Netherlands

Tall Dutch Egg Nog

Ingredients

Glass: 300mL/10oz Beer Mug
Mixers: 30mL/1fl oz Bacardi
30mL/1fl oz orange juice
10mL/⅜fl oz dark rum
10mL/⅜fl oz Advocaat
120mL/4fl oz milk

Method

Blend over ice. Garnish with a sprinkle of cinnamon and egg.

Tennessee Manhattan Dry

U.S.A.

Ingredients

Glass: 90mL/3oz Cocktail Glass
Mixers: 45mL/1½fl oz Tennessee whiskey
20mL/⅝fl oz dry vermouth
2 dashes Angostura Bitter

Method
Stir and strain into cocktail glass. Garnish with twist of lemon peel and serve.

Tennessee Sour

U.S.A.

Ingredients

Glass: 150mL/5oz Cocktail Glass
Mixers: 60mL/2fl oz Tennessee whiskey
juice ½ lemon
dash of sugar syrup
soda water (top up)

Method
Shake ingredients except soda water. Strain into cocktail glass, top with soda. Garnish with lemon slice and cherry and serve.

Mexico

Tequila Slammer

Ingredients
Glass: 185mL/6oz Old Fashioned
Mixers: 30mL/1fl oz tequila
30mL/1fl oz dry ginger ale

Method
Build, no ice.
A one hit wonder - holding a coaster over the entire rim, rotate the glass clockwise on the bar 4-5 times. Lift and 'slam' the base of the glass down onto the bar, then drain in one shot. The carbonated mixer fizzes the tequila when slammed.
Usually bartenders splash only 5-10mL/⅛-⅜fl oz of dry ginger ale to aid the quick drinking process.

Tequila Sunrise

Mexico

Ingredients

Glass: 285mL/9½oz Hi-Ball Glass
Mixers: 30mL/1fl oz tequila
5mL/⅛fl oz Grenadine
top-up with orange juice

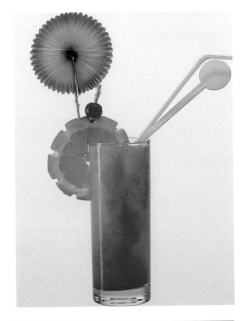

Method

Build over ice.
Sipping this long, cool cocktail at sunrise or sunset is magnificient.
To obtain the cleanest visual effect, drop Grenadine down the inside of the glass, after topping up with orange juice.
Dropping Grenadine in the middle creates a fallout effect, detracting from the presentation of the cocktail.
Best served with chilled, freshly squeezed oranges.

Tequila Sparkle

U.S.A.

Ingredients

Glass: 140mL/5oz Margarita Glass
Mixers: 20mL/⅝fl oz tequila
75mL/2½fl oz milk
30mL/1fl oz coffee liqueur
75mL/2½fl oz cream

Method

Frost the rims of a margarita glass with salt. Stir ingredients and strain into prepared glass and serve.

The Big Chill

Bermuda

Ingredients

Glass: 300mL/10oz Hi-Ball Glass
Mixers: 30mL/1fl oz Midori
30mL/1fl oz bacardi rum
15mL/½fl oz banana liqueur
90mL/3fl oz pineapple juice

Method

Build ingredients over ice in hi-ball glass and serve with straws.

Netherlands

The Dik Hewitt

Ingredients
Glass: 150mL/5oz Cocktail Glass
Mixers: 30mL/1fl oz Tennessee
           whiskey
           30mL/1fl oz cognac
           30mL/1fl oz Benedictine
           glass of water (on the side)

Method
Shake with ice and strain.

The Time Warp

Australia

Ingredients

Glass: 150mL/5oz Cocktail Glass
Mixers: 20mL/⅝fl oz Midori
           5mL/⅛fl oz Blue Curaçao
           15mL/½fl oz Malibu
           15mL/½fl oz pineapple juice
           5mL/⅛fl oz raspberry
           cordial

Method
Shake Midori, Malibu, pineapple juice
and strain into cocktail glass. Add
raspberry cordial and Blue Curaçao,
garnish with cherry and serve.

Third Degree

Saudi Arabia

Ingredients

Glass: 150mL/5oz Champagne
           Saucer
Mixers: 90mL/3fl oz gin
           10mL/⅜fl oz Pernod
           30mL/1fl oz dry vermouth

Method
Shake and strain into a champagne
saucer, garnish with lemon peel and
serve.

293

Third Rail

Italy

Ingredients

Glass: 90mL/3oz Cocktail Glass
Mixers: 30mL/1fl oz rum
20mL/⅝fl oz orange juice
20mL/⅝fl oz dry vermouth
20mL/⅝fl oz sweet
vermouth

Method

Shake and strain into cocktail glass
and serve.

Three Sisters

Australia

Ingredients

Glass: 150mL/5oz Champagne
Saucer
Mixers: 45mL/1½fl oz brandy
1 dash Grenadine
45mL/1½fl oz Galliano
45mL/1½fl oz orange juice

Method

Shake and strain into a champagne
saucer, garnish with cherry and serve.

Time Out

Indonesia

Ingredients

Glass: 285mL/9oz Fancy Hi-Ball
Glass
Mixers: 30mL/1fl oz brandy
30mL/1fl oz Kahlúa
60mL/2fl oz orange juice
30mL/1fl oz cream
peaches
dash of Grenadine

Method

Blend with ice and pour.

U.S.A.

Tom Collins

Ingredients

Glass: 140mL Champagne Saucer
Mixers: 60mL/2fl oz lemon juice
60mL/2fl oz gin
soda water

Method
Put cracked ice, lemon juice, soda water and gin in a glass. Fill with soda water and stir. Serve with a slice of lemon and cherry for garnish.
Brandy, bourbon, rum or any whisky can be used instead of gin, the Collins is named after the liqour used, eg. Rum Collins.

---

2 B Slippery

Australia

Ingredients
Glass: 180mL/6oz Old Fashioned
Mixers: 30mL/1fl oz black Sambucca
30mL/1fl oz lime cordial

Method
Build over ice.

Top of the Crop

France

Ingredients

Glass: 300mL/10oz Hi-Ball Glass
Mixers: 30mL/1fl oz Pernod
ginger beer (top up)
30mL/1fl oz Blue Curaçao

Method

Quarter fill a hi-ball glass with cracked ice. Add Pernod and Blue curaçao, top with ginger beer, add straws and serve.

Topping

United Kingdom

Ingredients

Glass: 90mL/3oz Cocktail Glass
Mixers: 30mL/1fl oz gin
30mL/1fl oz dry vermouth
1 Maraschino cherry
15mL/½fl oz Crème de Violette

Method

Shake and strain into cocktail glass, garnish with cherry and serve.

Trader Vic's Rum Fizz

U.S.A.

Ingredients

Glass: 135mL/4½oz Tulip Champagne Glass
Mixers: 30mL/1fl oz dark rum
30mL/1fl oz lemon juice
10mL/⅜fl oz sugar
15mL/½fl oz cream soda
1 raw egg

Method

Shake over ice and pour. Garnish with an orange spiral.
From the range of cocktails for which the internationally renowned cocktail bar proprietor has become recognised.

Australia

Traffic Light

Ingredients
Glass: Tall Dutch Cordial
Mixers: 20mL/⅞fl oz strawberry liqueur
10mL/⅜fl oz Galliano
10mL/⅜fl oz green Chartreuse

Method
Layer in order, light, then straw shoot.

Traffic Stopper

India

Ingredients
Glass: Whiskey Shot
Mixers: 15mL/½fl oz banana liqueur
15mL/½fl oz Blue Curaçao
15mL/½fl oz Baileys Irish
Cream

Method
Layer in order in a shot glass and
serve.

Transplant

Mauritius

Ingredients
Glass: 300mL/10oz Hi-Ball Glass
Mixers: 30mL/1fl oz Bacardi rum
10mL/⅜fl oz Galliano
10mL/⅜fl oz Crème de
Menthe
orange juice (top up)

Method
Place ingredients into a hi-ball glass
and top with orange juice. Garnish with
orange peel, straws and serve.

Triple Bypass

Portugal

Ingredients
Glass: 90mL/3oz Cocktail Glass
Mixers: 20mL/⅝fl oz Crème de Cassis
20mL/⅝fl oz white Crème de Menthe
20mL/⅝fl oz cherry brandy

Method
Layer liqueurs in order then float with cream.

Travelex

Austria

Ingredients
Glass: 90mL/3oz Cocktail Glass
Mixers: 20mL/⅝fl oz kümmel liqueur
15mL/½fl oz lemon juice
15mL/½fl oz Galliano
10mL/⅜fl oz vodka
10mL/⅜fl oz Crème de Banana

Method
Shake and strain into a cocktail glass, garnish with pineapple spear and serve.

Tropical

Philippines

Ingredients
Glass: 300mL/10oz Hi-Ball Glass
Mixers: 30mL/1fl oz vodka
60mL/2fl oz pineapple juice
30mL/1fl oz peach tree
1 dash cream
15mL/½fl oz Rubis
5 strawberries

Method
Blend and pour into hi-ball glass, add straws and serve.

Jamaica

Tropical Ambrosia

Ingredients
Glass: 285mL/9½oz Footed Hi-Ball
            Glass
Mixers: 1 mandarin orange
            1 apple
            150mL/5oz coconut milk
            15mL/½fl oz lemon juice

Method
Blend over ice and pour. Garnish with an apple slice.

Tropical Delight

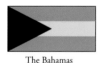

The Bahamas

Ingredients
Glass: 90mL/3oz Cocktail Glass
Mixers: 30mL/1fl oz dark rum
            30mL/1fl oz cream
            20mL/⅝fl oz orange juice

Method
Shake and strain into a cocktail glass, sprinkle with nutmeg and serve.

Tropical Field

U.S.A.

Ingredients
Glass: 150mL/5oz Cocktail Glass
Mixers: 30mL/1fl oz strawberry
            liqueur
            15mL/½fl oz cherry brandy
            30mL/1fl oz pineapple juice
            30mL/1fl oz cream

Method
Shake and strain into cocktail glass, garnish with strawberry, cherry and serve.

Australia

Tropical Itch

Ingredients

Glass: 425mL/14oz Hurricane Glass
Mixers: 45mL/1½fl oz rum
           45mL/1½fl oz bourbon
           juice of half fresh lime
           dash Angostura Bitter
           top-up with pineapple juice and
           passionfruit
           30mL/1fl oz rum, floated

Method
Build over ice.

Tropical Paradise

Cayman Is

Ingredients

Glass: 90mL/3oz Cocktail Glass
Mixers: 45mL/1½fl oz Bacardi rum
           5mL/⅛fl oz lemon juice
           45mL/1½fl oz peach tree
           1 slice mango
           20mL/⅝fl oz mango liqueur
           1 dash mango nectar

Method
Blend and pour into cocktail glass and
serve.

Tropical Sunset

Argentina

Ingredients

Glass: 300mL/10oz Hi-Ball Glass
Mixers: 30mL/1fl oz Bacardi rum
           60mL/2fl oz orange juice
           20mL/⅝fl oz Grand Marnier
           1 egg yolk
           30mL/1fl oz pineapple juice
           1 dash Grenadine

Method
Shake and strain into a hi-ball glass,
garnish with pineapple slice, straws
and serve.

Turkish Delight

Turkey

Ingredients
Glass: 285mL/9½ oz Hi-Ball Glass
Mixers: 30mL/1fl oz Sabra
              5mL/⅛fl oz Grenadine
              15mL/½fl oz Parfait Amour
              30mL/1fl oz cream
              120mL/4fl oz milk

Method
Shake and strain into a colada glass, sprinkle with chocolate flakes, add straws and serve.

Twilight Zone

U.S.A.

Ingredients
Glass: 150mL/5oz Champagne Saucer
Mixers: 60mL/2fl oz Bacardi rum
              15mL/½fl oz fresh cream
              30mL/1fl oz Crème de Menthe
              15mL/½fl oz Parfait Amour
              15mL/½fl oz lime cordial

Method
Shake and strain into a champagne saucer and serve.

Finland

Two Stroke

Ingredients
Glass: Cordial (Embassy)
Mixers: 30mL/1fl oz chilled vodka
              cracked pepper

Method
Layer in order.

V-Bomb

Poland

Ingredients

Glass: 300mL/10oz Beer Glass
Mixers: 60mL/2fl oz vodka
           15mL/½fl oz lemon juice
           sparkling wine

Method

Build over ice.

Valencia Smile

Spain

Ingredients

Glass: 150mL/5oz Champagne
           Flute
Mixers: 30mL/1fl oz apricot brandy
           30mL/1fl oz orange juice
           4 dashes apricot brandy
           Champagne (top up)

Method

Shake and strain into a flute glass, top
with champagne and serve.

Vampire's Passion

Romania

Ingredients

Glass: 150mL/5oz Cocktail Glass
Mixers: 30mL/1fl oz red Crème de
           Menthe
           30mL/1fl oz black
           Sambucca
           30mL/1fl oz Sambucca
           30mL/1fl oz Baileys
           Irish Cream
           15 mL (1/2 oz) strawberry
           liqueur

Method

Layer in order in cocktail glass and
serve.

Australia

Velvet Hue

Ingredients
Glass: 210mL/7oz Old Fashioned
Mixers: 30mL/1fl oz Brandy
           30mL/1fl oz Kahlúa
           30mL/1fl oz Cointreau
           90mL/3fl oz cream

Method
Shake with ice, then strain into glass.

Velvet Hammer

U.S.A.

Ingredients
Glass: 150mL/5oz Cocktail Glass
Mixers: 30mL/1fl oz Cointreau
           30mL/1fl oz cream
           30mL/1fl oz Galliano

Method
Half fill a cocktail glass with crushed ice. Shake ingredients, pour over ice and serve.

Vermouth Cassis

France

Ingredients
Glass: 180mL/8oz Wine Goblet
           Glass
Mixers: 90mL/3fl oz dry vermouth
           soda water (top up)
           45mL/1½fl oz Crème de
           Cassis

Method
Place a few cubes of ice in a goblet glass along with vermouth and Crème de Cassis. Top with soda water, garnish with lemon peel and serve.

Vicious Vernon

Chile

Ingredients

Glass: Whiskey Shot
Mixers: 15mL/½fl oz banana liqueur
          15mL/½fl oz Baileys Irish
          Cream
          15mL/½fl oz Kahlúa

Method
Layer in a shot glass and serve.

Violet Slumber

Czech Republic

Ingredients

Glass: 140mL Champagne
          Saucer
Mixers: 15mL/½fl oz Malibu
          10mL/⅜fl oz orange juice
          15mL/½fl oz Parfait Amour

Method
Layer in a shot glass and serve.

Viking II

Norway

Ingredients
Glass: Whisky Prism Shot
Mixers: 20mL/⅞fl oz Galliano
          20mL/⅞fl oz Aquavit

Method
Layer in order.

Water Bubba

Ivory Coast

Ingredients

Glass: Cordial (Embassy)
Mixers: 10mL/½fl oz cherry
Advocaat
10mL/½fl oz Blue Curaçao
10mL/⅜fl oz Advocaat

Method
Layer in order, serve.

Westmooreland

U.S.A.

Ingredients

Glass: 210mL/7oz Old Fashioned
Mixers: 90mL/3fl oz bourbon
1 tablespoon sugar
2 mint sprigs

Method
Crush half the mint with sugar and ice.
Place in an old fashioned glass, add
bourbon. Place remaining mint and ice
into glass and serve with straws.

Barbados

West Indies Yellow Bird

Ingredients

Glass: 210mL/ Footed Hi-Ball Glass
Mixers: 30mL/1fl oz dark rum
15mL/½fl oz Banana Liqueur
15mL/½fl oz Galliano
45mL/1½fl oz pineapple juice
45mL/1½fl oz orange juice

Method
Blend with ice. Garnish with a pineapple
wedge and cherry.

Wet Spot

Hong Kong

Ingredients

Glass: 150mL/5 oz Cocktail Glass
Mixers: 30mL/1fl oz Midori
         15mL/½fl oz Frangelico
         30mL/1fl oz apple juice
         30mL/1fl oz cream
         30mL/1fl oz passionfruit pulp,
         float

Method
Shake and strain all ingredients with the exception of passionfruit pulp. Pour into glass then float passionfruit pulp.

United Kingdom

Whiskey Sour

Ingredients
Glass: 140mL/5 oz Wine Glass
Mixers: 45mL/1½fl oz Scotch Whisky
         30mL/1fl oz lemon juice
         15mL/½fl oz sugar syrup
         ½ egg white

Method
Shake with ice and strain.
Garnish with a red cherry at bottom of glass and slice of lemon on side.
A quaint appetizer before dinner. Shake vigorously so the egg white rises to a frothy head after straining. Some people prefer a 140mL/5 oz cocktail glass.

Japan

Whisper

Ingredients

Glass: 390mL/13oz Poco Grande Glass

Mixers: 45mL/1½fl oz strawberry liqueur
45mL/1½fl oz mango liqueur
45mL/1½fl oz lime juice
45mL/1½fl oz lemon juice
peaches

Method
Blend with ice and strain.

White Lady

U.S.A.

Ingredients
Glass: 90mL/3oz Cocktail Glass
Mixers: 30mL/1fl oz gin
15mL/½fl oz lemon juice
15mL/½fl oz sugar syrup
½ egg white

Method
Shake with ice and strain. A traditional pre dinner cocktail. Pure yet bland, change to either:
"Blue Lady" - substitute Blue Curaçao for sugar syrup.
or "Pink Lady" - substitute Grenadine for sugar syrup and add cream.

Widow's Kiss

Luxembourg

Ingredients

Glass: 90mL/3oz Cocktail Glass
Mixers: 30mL/1fl oz apple brandy
10mL/⅜fl oz Benedictine
10mL/⅜fl oz yellow Chartreuse
5mL/⅛fl oz Angostura Bitter

Method
Shake over ice and strain. Garnish with a floating strawberry.

U.S.A.

Woodstock

Ingredients

Glass: 150mL/5oz Old Fashioned, sugar rimmed with maple syrup
Mixers: 30mL/1fl oz gin
10mL/⅜fl oz lemon juice
10mL/⅜fl oz maple syrup
2 dashes Angostura Bitter

Method
Shake over ice and strain, then add cubed ice. Garnish with a straw.

Australia

X.T.C.

Ingredients
Glass: 90mL/3oz Cocktail Glass
Mixers: 30mL/1fl oz Tia Maria
             30mL/1fl oz strawberry liqueur
             30mL/1fl oz cream

Method
Shake with ice and strain.
Butterfly strawberry placed on side of glass, twirl thickened cream over strawberry and sprinkle over flaked chocolate.

Yorker

U.S.A.

Ingredients
Glass: 180mL/6oz Colada Glass
Mixers: 30mL/1fl oz Midori
             30g/1oz avocado
             30mL/1fl oz cream
             60mL/2fl oz milk

Method
Blend ingredients and pour into a colada glass. Garnish with a strawberry and serve.

Zandoria

Jamaica

Ingredients
Glass: 140mL Champagne
             Saucer
Mixers: 30mL/1fl oz brandy
             30mL/1fl oz Tia Maria
             120mL/4fl oz fresh cream

Method
Shake and strain into cocktail glass.
Sprinkle with nutmeg and serve.

Zed

Belgium

Ingredients

Glass: 90mL/3oz Cocktail Glass
Mixers: 30mL/1fl oz gin
1 teaspoon sugar
30mL/1fl oz Mandarin
Napoleon
90mL/3fl oz pineapple juice

Method
Shake and strain into cocktail glass.
Garnish with mint sprig and lemon.

Zipper

U.S.A.

Ingredients

Glass: Cordial (Lexington)
Mixers: 10mL/⅜fl oz tequila
10mL/⅜fl oz Grand Marnier
10mL/⅜fl oz Baileys Irish
Cream

Method
Layer in order in a shot glass
and serve.

Zombie

Ivory Coast

Ingredients

Glass: 300mL/10oz Fancy Cocktail
Glass
Mixers: 45mL/1½fl oz Bacardi
30mL/1fl oz dark rum
30mL/1fl oz light rum
30mL/1fl oz pineapple juice
15mL/½fl oz lime or lemon
juice
30mL/1fl oz apricot brandy
5mL/⅛fl oz sugar syrup

Method
Shake with ice and pour.
Garnish: Pineapple spear and leaves,
cherry and mint leaves, swizzle stick and
straws.

Zoom

Portugal

Ingredients

Glass: 150mL/5oz Cocktail Glass
Mixers: 45mL/1½fl oz brandy
20mL/⅝fl oz cream
15mL/½fl oz honey

Method

Shake and strain into a cocktail glass and serve.

Zorba the Greek

Greece

Ingredients

Glass: 150mL/5oz Cocktail Glass
Mixers: 60mL/2fl oz Bacardi rum
30mL/1fl oz orange juice
15mL/½fl oz ouzo
15mL/½fl oz Grenadine

Method

Shake and strain into a cocktail glass and serve.

Zimbabwe

Zulu Warrior

Ingredients

Glass: 210mL/7oz Old Fashioned
Mixers: 30mL/1fl oz Midori
30mL/1fl oz strawberry liqueur
30mL/1fl oz lemon juice
strawberries
rockmelon

Method

Blend with ice and pour.

Cocktail Index

A

Aberdeen Angus 48

Abbey 48

ABC 48

Absolut Cosmopolitan 49

Abortion 49

Absinth 49

Acapulco 50

Acapulco I 50

Admiral Cannon 50

African Nipple 51

After Eight 51

Alabama Slammer 51

Alaska 52

Alexander 52

Alfonso 52

Alice in Wonderland 53

Alice 53

All Night 53

Almond Orange frost 54

Almond Joy 54

Altered States Shooter 54

Amaretto Choco Cream 55

Amaretto Sour 55

Amaretto Stinger 55

Americano 56

American Beauty 56

Amsterdam 56

Anabolic Steroid 57

Angel Dew 57

Andy Williams 57

Angel's Kiss 58

Angelique 58

Angry Fijian 58

Apple Buck 59

Appease Me 59

Apple Magic 59

Apres Ski 60

Apricot Smoothie 60

Aqua Thunder 60

Aquavit fiz 61

Argyle Tavern 61

Aspiration 61

Atomic Bomb 62

Astronaut 62

Aussie Slinger 62

Australian Gold 63

Autumn Leaf 63

Avalanche 63

B

B & B 64

B & G 64

B & P 64

Bacardi Blossom 65

Bacardi No. 2 65

Badminton 65

Bahama Mama 66

Baileys Coconut Cream 66

Ballet Russe 66

Baltimore Zoo 67

Bamboo 67

Banana Bender 67

Banana Bliss 68

Banana-Choc Shake 68

Banana Colada 68

Banana Daiquiri 69

Banana Jaffa 69

Banana Margarita 69

Bananarama 70

Banger 70

Bango 70

Banshee 71

Banshee No. 2 71

Barley Punch 71

Bee Sting 72

Bellini 72

Bellini (frozen) 72

Belly Dancer	73	Boloshoi Punch	87
Ben's Play Lunch	73	Boilermaker	87
Berlin	73	Bombay	87
Bermuda Rose	74	Bombay Punch	88
Berlin Binge	74	Bondi Blue	88
Bessie & Jessie	74	Born to be Alive	88
Between the Sheets	75	Bosom Caresser	89
Bikini	75	Bosom Caresser No. 2	89
Bill Bailey	75	Bossa Nova	89
B-52	76	Boston Cream	90
Black Dream	76	Boston Cocktail	90
Black Forrest	76	Bourbon Banana	90
Blackjack	77	Brain Dead	91
Black on White	77	Brandy Boss	91
Black Opal	77	Brandy Alexander	91
Black Russian	78	Brandy Daisy	92
Black Velvet	78	Brandy Egg Nog	92
Black Widow	78	Brandy Ice	92
Blood and Sand	79	Brandy Snaps	93
Blood Bath	79	Brandy Riviera	93
Bloody Mary	79	Brandy Toddy	93
Blossom	80	Brazilian Monk	94
Blow Up	80	Brazilian Breakdance	94
Blow Job	80	Break Shooter	94
Blueberry Delight	81	Brittany	95
Blueberry Delight No. 2	81	Bronx	95
Blue Blazer	81	Brown Betty	95
Blue Day	82		
Blue Dove	82		
Blue French	82		

C

Blue Hawaii	83		
Blue Haze	83	Café Nero	96
Blue Heaven	83	Café Paris	96
Blue Lady	84	Café Royal	96
Blue Lagoon No. 2	84	Cameron Cannon	97
Blue Lagoon	84	Campino	97
Blue Train	85	Canadian Daisy	97
Blushing Berry	85	Candy Cane	98
Blunt Screwdriver	85	Cape Kennedy	98
Bobby Dazzler	86	Caper's Caper	98
Bobby Burns	86	Careless Whisper	99
Body Heat	86	Carlton	99

Caribbean Champagne 99
Champagne Cocktail 100
Cha Cha 100
Champagne Cocktail No. 2 100
Champagne St Moritz 101
Champagne Pick-Me-Up 101
Champagne Tory 101
Chastity Belt 102
Channel 64 102
Chee Chee 102
Cheeky Girl 103
Cheer 103
Cherries Jubilee 104
Cherry 104
Cherry Alexander 104
Cherry Bomb 105
Cheryl 105
Chi Chi 105
Chiquita 106
Chicago 106
Choc Mint 106
Chocolate Chip Mint 107
Chocolate Baby 107
Chocolate Chip 107
Cointreau Caipirinha 108
Columbia Skin 108
Columbus 109
Comfort Baby 109
Copenhagen Special 109

De Rigueur 113
Depth Charge 113
Deshler 113
Devil's Handbrake 114
Diplomat 114
Dirty Mother 114
Dizzy Blonde 115
Dizzy Whistle 115
Doctor Dangerous 115
Dog's Special 116
Double Blazer 116
Dolomint 116
Double Jeopardy 117
Dragon's Fire 117
Drambuie High 117
Dubonnet Cocktail 118
Dubonnet Fizz 118
Duke of Marlborough 119
Dunk 119
Dust Settler 119
Dyevtchka 120

E

El Burro 120
El Diablo 121
Eldorado 121
Electric Blue 121
Esme's Peril 122
Eton Blazer 122
Evergreen 122

D

Daiquiri 110
Daiquiri - American 110
Daiquiri - Kings 111
Daiquiri - Kiwifruit 111
Daiquiri - Mango 111
Daiquiri - Strawberry 111
Death in the Afternoon 112
Death by Chocolate 112
Deep Throat 112

F

Fair Lady 123

Falcon's Delight 123

Fallen Angel 123

Firemans Sour 124

Fizz 124

Fjord 124

Flaming Sambucca 125

Flirt with Dirt 125

Flower 125

Fluffy Duck No. 1 126

Fluffy Duck No. 2 126

Flying Carpet 127

Flying High 127

Flying Dutchman 127

Fog Cutter 128

Forty Winks 128

Forth of July 128

401 129

Fraise Année 129

Franjelico Luau 129

Frappe 130

Frappe Byrrh 130

Frappe -Crème de Menthe 131

Frappe -Grand Marnier 131

Frappe-Midori & Cointreau 131

Frappe -Southern Peach 131

Freddy Fud Pucker 132

French 69 132

French 75 132

French Connection 133

French Fantasy 133

French Greenery 133

French Safari 134

Froth & Bubble 134

Frisco Sour 134

Frozen Aquavit 135

Frozen Guava Daiquiri 135

Frozen Leango 135

Frozen Mudslide 136

Fruit Passion 136

Fruit Salad 136

G

Galliano Hot Shot 137

Garden City 137

Geisha 137

Geisha Delight 138

Genoa 138

Georgia Peach 138

German Chocolate Cake 139

Get Going 139

Ghetto Blaster 139

Gibson 140

Gigolo's Delight 140

Gilroy 140

Gimlet 141

Gin and It 141

Gin and Sin 141

Gin Twist 142

Ginger Sin 142

Ginger Mick 142

Girl Talk 143

Globe Gladness 143

Glasgow 143

Godfather 144

Goddaughter 144

Godmother 144

Gold Passion 145

Golden 145

Golden Cadillac 145

Golden Dream 146

Golden Dream No. 2 146

Golden Dragon 146

Golden Orchid 147

Golden Shot 147

Golden Slipper 147

Gomango 148

Gone Troppo 148

Grand Baileys 148

Grasshopper 149

Gravedigger 149

Great White North 149

Greek Buck 150

Greek God 150

Green Back 150

Green 151

Green Devil 151

Green Eyes 152

Green Paradise 152

Green Slime 152

Green With Envy 153

Green Slammer 153

Greenhorn 153

Greenpeace Sorbet 154

Gringo 154

Gypsy King 154

H

Hair of the Dog 155

Hairless Duck 155

Half Nelson 155

Halo 156

Harbour Mist 156

Harbour Lights 156

Hard On 157

Hard On (Bloody) 157

Hard On (Black) 157

Harvey Wallbanger 158

Harlequin 158

Havana Club 158

Hawaiian Punch 159

Hazy Cuban 159

Head Stud 159

Health Farm 160

Heartbraker 160

Helen's Hangover 160

Hellraiser 161

Hemmingway 161

Highland Flying 161

Honey Bee 162

Honeyed Nuts 162

Honey Tea 162

Horangi 163

Horse Guards 163

Hot Buttered Rum 163

Hot Danish Cider 164

Hot Milk Punch 164

Hot Whiskey Toddy 165

Hurricane 165

I

I Love You 166

Ice Wings 166

Ice Kachany 166

Ichigo 167

Illusion 167

Independence Day Punch 167

Indo Shiner 168

Ink Street 168

Inkahlúarable 168

Intimate 169

Irish Eyes 169

Irish Coffee 169

Irish Flag 170

Iron Lady 170

Island Cooler 170

Italian Cocktail 171

Italian Streaker 171

J

Jack in the Box 172

Jack Rose 172

Jaffa 172

Japanese Slipper 173

Japanese Sunrise 173

Jaw Breaker 173

Jealous June 174

Jellybean (Garbos) 174
Jellybean 174
Jellyfish 175
Jeune Homme 175
Jersey Cow 175
Joburg 176
Joggers 176
John Collins 176
Jungle Stern 177
Jungle Juice 177
Jupiter Martini 177

K

Kahlúa Jaffa 178
Kakuri 178
Kamikaze 178
Ketango 179
Keep Going 179
Kelly's Comfort 179
K.G.B 180
Kick in the Balls 180
Kings Cross Nut 181
Kir Royale 181
Kir 181
Kiwi 182
Kiss My Asteroid 182
Klu Klux Klanger 182

L

Lady Brown 183
Lady in Red 183
Lady M 183
Lady Throat Killer 184
Lady's Pleasure 184
Lambada 184
Lamborghini 185
Lamborghini (Flaming) 185
Last Emperor 186
Last Straw 186
Lavender 186
Lena 187
Leonardo de Mango 187
Leprechaun 187
Lip Sip Suck 188
Lieutenant 188
Light Fingers 188
Lights of Havana 189
Lime Spider 189
Lion D'or 189
Lone Star 190
Long Green 190
Long Island Iced Tea 190
Long Neck 191
Love Dori 191
Louisiana Lullaby 191
Love Potion No. 9 192
Lucy's Lament 192
Lynchburg Lemonade 192

M

Macauley 193
Macleay Street 193
Madam Butterfly 193
Madras 194
Magnolia Blossom 194
Mai-Tai 194

Maiden's Blush	195
Malibu Sting	195
Malibu Magic	195
Mama Rosa	196
Mandarin Sling	196
Manhattan	197
Mango Lantis	197
Maples	197
Macroni	198
Mardi Gras	198
Margarita	198
Martini	199
Martin Luther King	199
Mary Queen of Scots	199
Melon Avalanche	200
Melon Ball	200
Melon Rock	200
Melon Tree	201
Merry Widow	201
Ménage à Trois	201
Metropolis	202
Mexican Berry	202
Mexican Flag	202
Mexican Madness	203
Mexican Mango	203
Mexican Runner	203
Miami Advice	204
Midnight Rose	204
Michaelangelo	204
Midnight Sax	205
Midori Alexander	205
Midori Colada	205
Midori Mist	206
Midori Splice	206
Mint Julep	206
Mintlup	207
Miss Aileen	207
Mission Impossible	207
Mississippi Mud	208
Mocha Mint	208
Mockatini	208
Molfetta Madness	209

Monk's Madness	209
Monkey Gland	209
Monkey's Punch	210
Monte Carlo	210
Montmartre	211
Moomba	211
Moonbeam	211
Moon Crater	212
Morning Glory	212
Moroccan Cocktail	212
Moscow Mule	213
Moulin Rouge	213
Mount Cook Sunset	213
Mount Temple	214
Mount Fuji	214
Myra	214

N

Napolean	215
New Yorker	215
Negroni	215
Nick's Health Drink	216
Nickel Fever	216
Night of Passion	216
Noah's Ark	217
Norman Conquest	217
Nude Bomb	217
Nutty Irishman	218

O

Oceanic	218
Off the Leach	218
Oil Fever	219
Old Pal	219
Old Fashioned - Scotch	219
Old San Fransisco	220
Ole	220
Opal Royale	220

Oppenheim Cocktail 221
Orange Blossom 221
Orange Bus 221
Orange Nog 222
Oramato 222
Orgasm 223
Orgasm Shooter 223
Oyster Shooter 224
Outer Space 224

P

Pablo 224
Paddy's Peril 225
Paint Box 225
Pago Pago 225
Palm Sundae 226
Palm Tree 226
Palomino 226
Papaya Sling 227
Paradise 227
Paris By Night 227
Paris Beach 228
Passionate Scene 228
Passionate 228
Peach Almond Shake 229
Peach Bomb 229
Peach Explosion 229
Peach Magic 230
Peach Marnier 230
Peach Me 230
Pearl Necklace 231
Pearl Harbour 231
Petite Fleur 231
Photo Finish 232
Piaff 232
Picadilly Punch 232
Picasso 233
Pickled Brain 233
Pick-Me-Up 233
Pimms No. 1 Cup 234

Piña Colada 234
Pinchgut Peril 235
Pineapple Bomber 235
Pineapple Plantation 235
Pink Angel 236
Pink Elephant 236
Pink Gin 236
Pink Panther 237
Pink Lady 237
Pink Pussy 237
Pipsqueak 238
Pirates Plunder 238
P. J. 238
Plantation Night 239
Playground 239
Planters Punch 239
Polish Sidecar 240
Polynesia 240
Port in a Storm 241
Porto Flip 241
Prairie Oyster 241
Pretty Woman 242
Prince of Wales 242
Purple Shell 243
Purple Waters 243
P.S. I Love You 243
Puerto Rican Pink Lady 244
Purple People Eater 244

Q

Quebec 245
Queen Bee 245
Queen Elizabeth 245
Queen's Peg 246
Queen's 246
Quenchie 246

R

R & R 247
Rabbit's Revenge 247
Rabbit-Punch 247
Raffles Singapore Sling 248
Raging Bull 248
Raider 248
Rasputins Revenge 249
RAM 249
Ramona 249
Rasputin's Revenge 250
Ray Long 250
Ready, Set, Go! 250
Red Eye 251
Red Cucumber Bowl 251
Red Lights 251
Rendezvous 252
Rhett Butler 252
Rhythm of Love 252
Rio Lady 253
Ritz 253
Rob Roy 253
Rock Lobster 254
Rocket Fuel 254
Rolls Royce 255
Roman Driver 255
Russian Tea 255
Rusty Bucket 256
Rusty Nail 256
Rusty Nail No. 2 256
Rusty Spade 257
Ryans's Rush 257

S

Sail Away 258
Saint Petersburg 258
Saint Moritz 258
Saint Vincent 259
Sake Special 259
Saketini 259
Salty Dog 260
Salubrious Salutations 260
Sambucca Shaker 260
Sangria 261
Satin Pillow 261
Saturday Night 262
Soyonara 262
Scandinavian Glogg 262
Scarlett O'Hara 263
Scorpian 263
Scotch Frog 264
Scotch Mate 264
Scotch Mist 264
Scotch Solace 265
Screaming Lizard 265
Screwdriver 265
Sea Breeze 266
Seduction 266
Sex on the Beach 266
Shady Lady 267
Shandy 267
Shanghai Punch 267
Sheep's Head 268
Sherry 268
Shirley Temple 268
Shocking Blue 269
Shooting Star 269
Short Leg 269
Sicilian Kiss 270
Sidecar 270
Simply Peaches 271
Sing Sing 271
Slippery Nipple 271

Slow Comfortable Screw 272
Slow Comfortable Screw No. 2 272
Slyde Your Thigh 272
Smog City 273
Smooth Boy 273
Snake in the Grass 273
Snake Bite Shooter 274
Snake Bite 274
Snoopy's Gleam 274
Snowball 275
Snow Drop 275
Snow Flake 275
Something Swampy 276
Sonja 276
South Pacific 276
South Seas 277
South Yarra Samurai 277
Southern Peach 277
Soviet Cocktail 278
Spanish Moss 278
Splice 279
Special Cream Chocolate 279
Springbok 279
Spritzer 280
Sputnik 280
Squashed Frog 280
Stars & Stripes 281
Steroid Blast 281
Stimulation 281
Stinger 282
Stormy Monday 282
Strawberry Blonde 283
Strawberry Colada 283
Strawberry Margarita 283
Strawberry Tongo 284
Strawgasm 284
Summer Breeze 284
Summer Sherbet 285
Sundancer 285
Sunken Treasure 285
Sunkissed 286
Sunset Special 286

Suntorian Star 286
Surfers Paradise 287
Surprise 287
Swedish Snowball 287
Sweet Lady Jane 288
Sweet Maria 288
Sweet Martini 289
Sweet Sixteen 289
Swiss Chocolate 289

T

Talisman 290
Temptation 290
Tall Dutch Egg Nog 290
Tennessee Manhattan Dry 291
Tennessee Sour 291
Tequila Slammer 291
Tequila Sunrise 292
Tequila Sparkle 292
The Big Chill 292
The Dik Hewitt 293
The Time Warp 293
Third Degree 293
Third Rail 294
Three Sisters 294
Time Out 294
Tickled Pink 295
T.N.T 295
Toblerone 296
Tokyo Joe 296
Tokyo Rose 296
Tom Collins 297
2 B Slippery 297
Top of the Crop 298
Topping 298
Trader Vic's Rum Fizz 298
Traffic Light 299
Traffic Stopper 299
Transplant 299
Triple ByPass 300

Travelex 300
Tropical 300
Tropical Ambrosia 301
Tropical Delight 301
Tropical Field 301
Tropical Itch 302
Tropical Paradise 302
Tropical Sunset 302
Turkish Delight 303
Twilight Zone 303
Two Stroke 303

V

V-Bomb 304
Valencia Smile 304
Vampire's Passion 304
Velvet Hue 305
Velvet Hammer 305
Vermouth Cassis 305
Vicious Vernon 306
Violet Slumber 306
Viking II 306
Virgin Mary 307
Virgin's Delight 307
Virgin's Paradise 307
Vodkatini 308
Vodka Gibson 308
Vodka Collins 308
Volcano 309
Voodoo Cure 309
Voodoo Child 309

W

Waldorf 310
Ward 310
Ward Eight 310
Water Bubba 311
Westmooreland 311
West Indies Yellow Bird 311
Wet Spot 312
Whiskey Sour 312
Whisper 313
White Lady 313
Widow's Kiss 314
Woodstock 314

X, Y, Z

X.T.C. 315
Yorker 315
Zandoria 315
Zed 316
Zipper 316
Zombie 316
Zoom 317
Zorba the Greek 317
Zulu Warrior 317